Wired for work?

ICT and job seeking in rural areas

Ronald W. McQuaid, Colin Lindsay and Malcolm Greig

JR
JOSEPH
ROWNTREE
FOUNDATION

The **Joseph Rowntree Foundation** has supported this project as part of its programme of research and innovative development projects, which it hopes will be of value to policy makers, practitioners and service users. The facts presented and views expressed in this report are, however, those of the authors and not necessarily those of the Foundation.

Joseph Rowntree Foundation
The Homestead
40 Water End
York YO30 6WP
Website: www. jrf.org.uk

First published 2003 by the Joseph Rowntree Foundation

A CIP catalogue record for this report is available from the British Library.

ISBN 1 85935 119 0 (paperback)
ISBN 1 85935 120 4 (pdf: available at www.jrf.org.uk)

Cover design by Adkins Design

Prepared and printed by:
York Publishing Services Ltd
64 Hallfield Road
Layerthorpe
York YO31 7ZQ
Tel: 01904 430033; Fax: 01904 430868; Website: www.yps-publishing.co.uk

Further copies of this report, or any other JRF publication, can be obtained either from the JRF website (www.jrf.org.uk/bookshop/) or from our distributor, York Publishing Services Ltd, at the above address.

Contents

Acknowledgements

We would like to acknowledge the valuable comments and advice provided by our JRF project advisory group: Mark Hinman, Joseph Rowntree Foundation; Professor John Farrington, School of Resources, Environment and Society, University of Aberdeen; Professor Andrew Gillespie, Centre for Urban and Regional Development Studies, University of Newcastle; Professor Brian Loader, Community Informatics Research and Applications Unit, University of Teeside; John Dennison, District Manager, Highlands and Western Isles, Jobcentre Plus; David Greaves, Policy Manager, Information and Social Strategy, West Lothian Council; Jim Logan, District Manager, Lothian and Borders, Jobcentre Plus (also Barbara McManus, Business Manager, Lothian and Borders, Jobcentre Plus); and Gordon Todd, Sutherland Area Development Manager, The Highland Council. Our thanks also go to Dr Martin McCracken, Employment Research Institute, Napier University who provided research support during both phases of the project. We are grateful for the support of the following agencies during the survey phase of the research: in West Lothian – West Lothian Council and Social Inclusion Partnership; in Wick and Sutherland – Caithness and Sutherland Enterprise, The Highland Council and the European Social Fund. In both study areas we were greatly assisted by the co-operation of Jobcentre Plus staff. We are also grateful for the help provided by Jobcentre Plus during the focus group phase of the research, along with the invaluable assistance provided by the following individuals: Diane Ross, West Highland College Programme Centre; Raewyn Black, West Lothian Council New Deal Unit; Tammy Davidson, Livingston Training Centre, West Lothian; Margaret Graham, Broxburn Family and Community Centre, West Lothian; Susan Walker, 'The Workplace', West Lothian. Finally, our thanks to all the job seekers who agreed to participate in the research.

Summary

Background and aims

Rural areas are, by definition, affected by their relative peripherality from industrial and population centres, and their dispersed patterns of economic and social activity. The geographical remoteness of many rural communities limits the availability of public services, which tend to be concentrated in highly populated areas. The scattered and sparsely populated settlements that are typical of many rural areas also generate specific practical and financial problems for public agencies charged with delivering services. As a result, policy makers are increasingly turning to Internet and other ICT-based approaches (such as telephone helplines) to deliver services. However, given that ICT access and use tends to be concentrated amongst more affluent and skilled people, concerns have been raised that ICT-based services will not be readily available to the most disadvantaged groups in society, potentially deepening their sense of exclusion.

This report seeks to discuss these issues, with specific reference to the current and potential role of ICT, and especially the Internet, in delivering job search services for unemployed people. We address two key questions facing policy makers and service providers tackling labour market disadvantage in both rural and urban areas:

- What are the potential benefits and barriers associated with the delivery of services for job seekers through the use of ICT-based systems, and particularly the Internet, in rural and other labour markets?
- What is the nature and extent of the 'digital divide' affecting unemployed job seekers and what policies are required to address this problem?

Study areas and methodology

The report is based on the findings of two phases of research and compares the experiences and attitudes of unemployed job seekers in two Scottish study areas: the adjacent Wick and Sutherland travel-to-work areas (TTWA) in the extreme northeast Highlands; and the centrally located West Lothian local authority area. These study areas provide a highly useful comparative framework: the first area includes Sutherland, a large, sparsely populated, remote rural TTWA, with small dispersed settlements and a population density amongst the lowest in Europe, and the neighbouring small rural town of Wick. The other study area, West Lothian, is a well-connected peri-urban local authority area, located near Edinburgh, in the heart of Scotland's 'central belt'.

The first phase of the research involved the comparative analysis of two pre-existing datasets. These datasets were developed as a result of commissioned research undertaken between November 2000 and May 2001 in the two study areas. Interviews (supplemented by limited postal survey exercises) were carried out with a random sample of unemployed job seekers in each area. In total, 300 responses were gathered in West Lothian, and 190 in Wick and Sutherland. The two datasets were harmonised for the purposes of this research. Quantitative analysis was undertaken using SPSS 10.0 for Windows. The second phase of the research was designed to follow up the issues raised by the quantitative data analysis. Retaining the original study areas, a series of 12 focus groups were held with job seekers between July and November 2002 (six in West Lothian, and three each in Wick and Sutherland), including one telephone-based focus group, conducted with job seekers residing in particularly remote areas of Sutherland.

Job seeking and the role of ICT: survey findings

The survey findings demonstrated that job seeking using advanced forms of ICT (namely the Internet) remains an activity of a minority of unemployed people, although contact with telephone helplines was an important job search method for those in remote areas. Access to and use of ICT was affected by a range of factors related to individual characteristics, personal circumstances, labour market geography and the availability of local services. There was evidence of a 'digital divide' affecting the most disadvantaged job seekers. Access and use of the Internet was more common amongst job seekers at the 'top end' of the scale in terms of educational attainment, household income group and ICT skills. Furthermore, young people and the long-term unemployed, exactly the client groups that can most struggle to access informal, social networks in the labour market, were also disadvantaged in terms of Internet access and use.

The geography of local labour markets, in combination with the availability of services, also appeared to have an important impact. Respondents in the remote rural Sutherland TTWA were much more likely to acknowledge the potential benefits of the Internet as a job search tool and were regular users of telephone helplines provided by Jobcentre Plus. Those living in areas served by Jobcentre facilities, such as West Lothian and Wick, appeared to be less likely to have regularly used ICT as a job search tool, and were also less likely to rely on informal social networks (crucial in remote rural areas) as a means of identifying job opportunities. It would seem that the combination of geographical remoteness and the absence of services 'on the ground' in Sutherland's more remote communities has helped lead to the growth of Internet use as a means of job seeking. As noted above, these job seekers were also much more likely to use telephone helplines provided by Jobcentre Plus. These findings suggest that the government's move towards ICT-based services may be welcomed by some job seekers, especially in remote rural areas. However, if these services are to be effective, action is required to address the digital divide, and link job search services to the informal networks governing rural job seeking.

Attitudes to ICT-based job seeking: focus group findings

The second phase of the research, carried out through focus groups, highlighted that job seekers can be adaptable when faced with the introduction of new services delivered via ICT. The introduction of computerised jobpoint terminals in Jobcentres was largely, though not universally, welcomed. Although some job seekers thought that the current design of the jobpoint software over-complicated the job search process and could be improved, most welcomed the autonomy and privacy afforded by the new system. Internet-based job seeking again emerged as of relatively marginal importance in most cases. Many lacked ICT skills and showed relatively limited awareness of the Internet. Focus group participants in rural Sutherland were much more likely to use the Internet to look for work than those in other areas, but even here there was scepticism as to whether web-based job seeking added value to existing job search services, mainly delivered via telephone helplines. Focus group participants in rural areas (both Wick and Sutherland) suggested that the depressed state of the local economy and the reliance of many employers and job seekers on informal networking limited the impact of any formal services, delivered via ICT or in person.

Telephone helplines were important to job seekers' activities in Sutherland, where the Jobcentre Plus agency has no local office facilities, and relies on telephone contact to provide information and advice services for its clients.

However, there were suggestions that the gradual replacement of a 'local' helpline service, provided by staff at Wick Jobcentre, with an increasing reliance on the centralised national telephone service, 'Jobseeker Direct', left many job seekers in Sutherland's remote communities frustrated by the lack of 'local knowledge' amongst helpline advisers. This issue highlighted the way in which the introduction of 'remote' ICT services can unintentionally increase the sense of isolation amongst vulnerable groups, with implications for the overall quality of services delivered by public agencies.

Conclusions and implications for research and policy

This report illustrates the importance of both labour market geography and personal characteristics and circumstances in affecting attitudes towards job seeking through ICT (and particularly the Internet). In the peri-urban West Lothian labour market, and even the remote town of Wick, unemployed people were less aware of, and experienced with, ICT-based job seeking, probably due to the accessibility of near-by Jobcentre facilities. In more remote communities where no such facilities are available, job seekers were more likely to use a range of ICT-based job search tools. However, there remained a clear digital divide, with more disadvantaged job seeker groups less likely to be able to exploit the opportunities afforded by advances in ICT. Those unemployed people with higher household incomes and who reported having good ICT skills were significantly more likely to have home access to the Internet. Conversely, young people (i.e. those in the 18–24 age group) and the long-term unemployed were significantly less likely to report home Internet access. There was also a statistically significant association between higher levels of educational attainment and ICT skills and the use of the Internet as a job search tool. Again, the young and the long-term unemployed were significantly less likely to use the Internet to look for work. In summary, those already disadvantaged in terms of skills, educational attainment and income are clearly less likely to have the access and skills required to benefit from using ICT (and particularly the Internet) as a job search tool. The shift towards ICT-based services risks leaving these individuals behind, unless they receive adequate training and support through accessible local services.

Yet while ICT-based job seeking (especially in the form of the use of Internet services) remains of relatively marginal importance at present, there may be opportunities for policy makers to promote new technologies as a means of widening access to both formal information and advice services and informal job search networks. There may be added value in the development of community-focused, web-based resources providing easy access to local job bulletins and interactive services such as e-mail vacancy updates and 'virtual spaces', where job seekers, employers and service providers can share information and interact on a less formal basis. In terms of formal information and services, there would be advantages in the development of more interactive job search sites, allowing job seekers to store search preferences and user profiles, and to follow through with identified vacancies by making on-line applications. At a more basic level, changes to the design of the web-based resources provided by Jobcentre Plus, to allow general browsing across occupations and areas, as well as geographically targeted searches, would be welcome. Similarly, the information provided on job opportunities should offer sufficient details on pay, conditions and location to enable job seekers to make an informed choice as to whether they wish to progress with an application.

However, unlocking the potential of the Internet as a job search tool may also rely on the provision of adequate community ICT facilities. Existing community resources have been successfully extended and converted for additional use as ICT centres in many areas. There may be benefits in seeking to encourage this trend, especially in rural areas without easily accessible Jobcentre facilities. Local community ICT facilities offering training and advice provided by professional project staff, alongside an emphasis on social interaction and peer support, may be able to combine the best elements of informal networking (so important in rural labour markets) and formal job search services.

Finally, there is a need for further research into the relationship between ICT access and use and job search success, and the most effective strategies for implementing ICT-based services in both urban and rural settings. Given the concerns raised by our research regarding the potential for 'remote' ICT-based services to add to the sense of exclusion felt by some vulnerable people in isolated areas, further research is also required into how best to balance services delivered through ICT and the Internet, with the need for local community facilities to support job seekers and others in rural areas.

1 Background and context

This chapter considers the general background to the study, the policy context and the study aims and methodology, and provides a description of the study areas.

Background to the study

Rural labour markets in the United Kingdom and across Europe have recently experienced a period of rapid and continuous change. Despite overall reductions in unemployment in recent years, relatively high unemployment (and particularly long-term unemployment) remains a persistent problem in many rural areas. Accordingly, a number of recent studies have sought to investigate the dynamics of the unemployment problem within these areas, resulting in the identification of a range of barriers to work faced by rural job seekers. These barriers include:

- demand-side problems related to industrial restructuring, geographical remoteness, and low population density
- localised skills mismatches
- an over-reliance on low-skilled, casualised, seasonal work
- the preponderance of small enterprises that are more likely to fall victim to sectoral downturns
- weak transport infrastructure and
- the importance of informal social networks that can exclude disadvantaged groups.[1]

Recent research has suggested that an important additional barrier to work faced by the unemployed in rural labour markets relates to the absence of locally-based job search and advice services, which are routinely provided by key public agencies in urban areas (Lindsay *et al.*, 2003). Jobcentre Plus, the main public agency dealing with unemployed job seekers, has argued that given the remote and sparsely populated nature of some rural labour markets, job search and advice services delivered through information and communication technologies (ICT) may offer a cost-effective policy solution (see Box 1 for definition). This report seeks to evaluate this claim, by analysing the extent to which job seekers (and especially groups particularly at risk of long-term exclusion from the labour market) are able to access and effectively use ICT-based services.

> **Box 1: Definition of 'ICT'**
>
> The term 'information and communication technologies' (ICT) has been used in a number of contexts. The OECD has defined ICT as 'information technology plus telecommunications equipment and services' (2000). This broad approach is adopted for the purposes of this report. ICT is defined as any computing and telecommunications hardware, applications software and services in the relevant policy area, specifically telephone, Internet or other computer-mediated tools or services. In practice, the report focuses on the use of telephone helplines, Internet websites and web-accessing computerised terminals ('jobpoints') located in Jobcentre offices.

The report is based on the findings of two phases of research, both comparing the experiences and attitudes of unemployed job seekers in two Scottish study areas: the combined Wick and Sutherland travel-to-work areas (TTWA); and the West Lothian local authority area. These study areas provide a highly useful comparative framework: Wick and Sutherland are remote rural areas (the former a small rural town, the latter a large and sparsely populated rural TTWA); West Lothian, on the other hand, is a well-connected local authority area located in the heart of Scotland's 'central belt'.

The policy context

Rural areas are, by definition, affected by their relative peripherality from industrial and population centres, and their dispersed patterns of economic and social activity. The geographical remoteness of many rural communities from major centres of economic activity clearly affects the availability of public services, which tend to be concentrated in highly populated areas of industrial development. The scattered and sparsely populated settlements that are typical of many rural areas also generate specific practical and financial problems for public agencies charged with delivering services. The potential benefits accruing from the use of remote, ICT-based services are therefore particularly apparent in more isolated rural communities, which are often characterised by weak physical service infrastructures, and where alternative forms of interaction can be expensive, time-consuming and infrequent.

As a result, policy makers are increasingly turning to Internet and other ICT-based approaches to delivering services, in the belief that: 'ICT can have a far-reaching impact on the quality of life of marginalised segments of the population, by providing more responsive and transparent governance as well as improving the reach and delivery of health, education and other social services' (ILO, 2001). In more general terms, it has also been suggested that the capacity of the Internet in particular to facilitate information sharing and individual participation can lead to the growth of more demand-responsive services from the 'bottom up'. Community-based Internet projects offering easy access to official public services, whilst also hosting alternative, independent information and discussion sites may be one positive outcome of the expansion of web-based provision.

However, despite a wave of 'techno-optimism' in the early 1990s, more recent analyses of ICT access and usage, in both urban and rural areas, suggest that claims that the Internet will inevitably result in the 'death of distance' as a barrier to employment and social inclusion are at best premature (Van Winden, 2001; Graham, 2002). The introduction of new technologies has generally tended to benefit the least disadvantaged, while large numbers of individuals continue to be excluded as a result of their educational or financial status. More affluent and skilled workers are much more likely to possess the skills, knowledge and financial resources to exploit fully the opportunities offered by the Internet and other technological advances. Nevertheless, policy makers at the regional, UK and European level remain convinced of the value of ICT in providing services, especially in rural areas (DEFRA, 2000; DTI, 2000; Scottish Executive, 2001b). The Scottish Executive's *Rural Scotland* policy document reflects a strong belief in the capacity of ICT to deliver 'high quality of life through access to services' in rural areas, although healthcare and education, rather than employment access, are its main focal points (Scottish Executive, 2000).

In the specific area of provision for the unemployed, the public employment service, Jobcentre Plus, has promoted its 'Internet job bank' and 'Jobseeker Direct' national telephone helpline as important supplementary services throughout the country, and as its primary means of contact with job seekers in remote rural areas. The development and expansion of telephone and Internet-based services is a core component of the agency's continuing reform programme, 'Modernising Employment Service'. The Jobcentre Plus website has provided job search services since November 2000. However, the website's database has also become familiar to job seekers using the national Jobcentre network, owing to the recent introduction of ICT-based systems into local offices in the form of computerised 'jobpoints'.

Between April 2001 and February 2002 Jobcentre Plus carried out a programme of modernisation within its offices, which saw 9,000 computerised 'jobpoints' installed in 1,007

Jobcentres nation-wide.[2] These touch-screen kiosks, which allow job seekers to carry out searches by area and occupation using the same national jobs database found on the organisation's website, have been introduced to replace the traditional system of 'cards and boards', which saw information summaries about job opportunities quite literally 'pinned to the wall'. While the introduction of jobpoints arguably marks a considerable step forward from this previous, rather basic way of displaying job information, concerns have been raised regarding the ability of some job seekers (who may have limited ICT skills) to fully exploit the new technology.

The 'Jobseeker Direct' national telephone helpline was launched as a pilot programme in January 1999, and following the pilot's extension became a permanent component of the agency's provision in March 2000. The helpline, which charges at local call rates, offers job search services to unemployed people or other members of the public seeking advice on employment opportunities. However, telephone-based services play an even more important role in one of our remote rural study areas. Given the absence of local, community-based Jobcentre facilities, unemployed people in many areas of rural Sutherland are not required to attend Jobcentres to carry out job search activities or 'sign on' as actively seeking work. Instead, these job seekers telephone their nearest local Jobcentre in Wick (using a free-phone number) in order to confirm their availability for work and receive job search advice. This service, although supplemented by the Jobseeker Direct national helpline and the Jobcentre Plus website, amounts to the public employment service's only regular contact with job seekers in these remote areas. The Jobcentre Plus agency's objective is to offer ICT-based provision that can, as far as possible, deliver the range and quality of information available to clients receiving face-to-face services at Jobcentre facilities in less remote labour markets.

Early evidence suggests that the web-based services offered by Jobcentre Plus tend to be viewed as user-friendly and helpful, but have not been associated with greater job search efficiency or success. Furthermore, research carried out for the Department for Work and Pensions has suggested that unemployed people are far less likely to have knowledge of the Internet than other members of the labour force, and that the long-term unemployed and those with poor work records tend to be particularly disadvantaged in this area (GHK, 2002a; Coleman *et al.*, 2002). Given these potential difficulties and the policy context discussed above, there is a need for further in-depth research into job seekers' experiences of and attitudes towards ICT and the Internet.

Aims and methods

The research discussed in this report sought to address two key questions facing policy makers and service providers tackling labour market disadvantage in both rural and urban areas:

- What are the potential benefits and barriers associated with the delivery of services for job seekers through the use of ICT-based systems, and particularly the Internet, in rural and other labour markets?
- What is the nature and extent of the 'digital divide' affecting unemployed job seekers and what policies are required to address this problem?

In seeking to contribute to this research agenda, the project pursued four main aims:

- To analyse the potential for ICT to be effectively used to deliver services for job seekers in rural and other areas, by examining individuals' skills levels and attitudes and access to the relevant technology.

- To analyse potential barriers to the use of ICT-based job seeking, and particularly those faced by disadvantaged and excluded groups (for example, older workers with little experience of new technologies, the long-term unemployed; and others on low incomes), and barriers to the delivery of services via ICT faced by key agencies.
- To identify area-based factors affecting the use of ICT as a job search tool, specifically comparing the experiences of job seekers in remote rural and peri-urban labour markets.
- To identify potential for policy action, reflecting the potential benefits and problems associated with the use of ICT-based job seeking facilities.

Within these aims, an implicit aspect of the study relates to the more general issue of the degree to which ICT-based services should reflect and facilitate individuals' current practices (i.e. their job search methods, for the purposes of this study), or should result in the re-engineering of service provision, thus directing or assisting people to 'do things differently'. ICT provides the opportunity to re-engineer: what the client does; the technology used by clients; how and what services are provided by key agencies; and how other organisations and individuals are linked or networked to existing services.

The report is based on the findings of two distinct phases of research: the first being a broad survey of unemployed people, and the second, a series of in-depth focus groups – with both phases comparing the experiences and attitudes of unemployed job seekers in the same two Scottish study areas.

The first phase involved the comparative analysis of two pre-existing datasets. These datasets were developed as a result of commissioned research undertaken between November 2000 and May 2001 in the two study areas: the West Lothian local authority area, and the contiguous Wick and Sutherland TTWAs. Survey research was carried out with a random sample of unemployed job seekers in each area. In total, 300 responses were gathered in West Lothian, and 190 in Wick and Sutherland. Although the vast majority of responses in both study areas were gathered through semi-structured, face-to-face interviews (424), these were supplemented by limited postal and telephone survey exercises (66). The two datasets were harmonised for the purposes of this research. Quantitative analysis was undertaken using SPSS 10.0 for Windows, with the results reported in Chapter 2 of this report. The analysis focused on respondents' access to and use of ICT, and on the relative importance of ICT and the Internet in job seeking activities.

The second phase was designed to follow up the issues raised by the quantitative data analysis. Retaining the original study areas, the second phase involved a series of focus groups with vulnerable job seekers who had experienced, or were at risk of, long-term exclusion from the active labour market. Twelve focus groups were convened (six in West Lothian, and three each in Wick and Sutherland) between July and November 2002. In total, 72 people contributed to focus group discussions. In the West Lothian study area, focus groups were constructed so as to target each of four key client groupings amongst the unemployed: the long-term unemployed (two focus groups); young people (two); women returners with children (one); and those aged over 50 (one). The limited populations in the Wick and Sutherland areas made it necessary to construct 'general' focus groups, not biased towards any particular client group, although in the event over half of respondents in this area were long-term unemployed, with approximately one-third aged over 50.

Focus groups were mainly held at community centres and other public facilities in the two study areas – participants were often users of community-based facilities offering services for job seekers at these locations, which in some cases included Internet-based provision. Each focus group involved 3–10 participants, who were selected on the basis that they were unemployed and looking for work. All participants were 'unemployed' using the internationally accepted definition used by the International Labour Organisation (ILO), although some were not claiming unemployment-related benefits and could not therefore be described as 'actively seeking work' under the Jobcentre Plus definition.[3] One focus group, with job seekers scattered across the remote Sutherland TTWA, was conducted via a telephone 'conference call'. Focus group discussions centred on participants' attitudes towards the Internet and other forms of ICT, their experiences of using ICT-based provision and other current services for the unemployed, and methods of looking for work.

The study areas

Although initially based on an analysis of two broad study areas, the research in fact provides a framework for comparing three types of geographical area: Sutherland is a large, remote and sparsely populated rural TTWA in the northern Scottish Highlands; Wick is a small, neighbouring, remote rural town; and West Lothian is a well-connected peri-urban area located near Edinburgh in the heart of Scotland's 'central belt'.

Caithness (the area in which Wick is located) and Sutherland are the most northerly counties of mainland Britain, and are therefore particularly remote from major centres of economic investment and industrial activity. The areas are also among the most sparsely populated in Europe (14.8 persons per km^2 in Caithness and only 2.2 persons per km^2 in Sutherland). Both areas have been affected by persistently high rates of unemployment and long-term unemployment. Within this general context, the Wick and Sutherland TTWAs face specific challenges as a result of industrial restructuring and the decline of traditional centres of employment. Wick (population approximately 8,000) is a small town struggling to cope with the impact of the restructuring of traditional fishing-related industries, whilst the more sparsely populated Sutherland TTWA (population approximately 13,000), covering an extensive geographical area of 5,865 km^2, has also been highly dependent on a now declining primary sector employment. With the decline of these traditional industries, tourism, financial services and public sector employment now dominate the limited opportunities within Wick and Sutherland.

As noted above, the services available to job seekers in these two sub-areas differ markedly. The Wick TTWA is dominated by the town of Wick, which has its own Jobcentre Plus office. The geographically much larger Sutherland TTWA hosts a number of very remote settlements, but has no physical Jobcentre facilities. As a result, unlike their counterparts in the Wick TTWA, many of Sutherland's job seekers are excused from the fortnightly routine of appearing in person at Jobcentres to 'sign on' as actively seeking work. This distinction is important. In most parts of the UK 'signing on' forms the basis for regular, compulsory attendance at Jobcentres by claimants. Although often seen as an expression of the public employment service's 'benefit policing' role, the routine of regular meetings with Jobcentre staff also provides unemployed people with an important focal point for job seeking activities and an opportunity to access information and advice (Lindsay *et al.*, 2003). The absence of formal services provided by Jobcentres is likely to impact on the job search strategies deployed by unemployed people, and may result in their readiness to adopt alternative methods, ranging from the use of ICT to a reliance on informal, social networks.

The second study area provides a strong contrast. The West Lothian local authority area (population approximately 157,000) is a peri-urban area situated in the central belt of Scotland,

Figure 1 Map: Location of Wick and Sutherland and West Lothian study areas

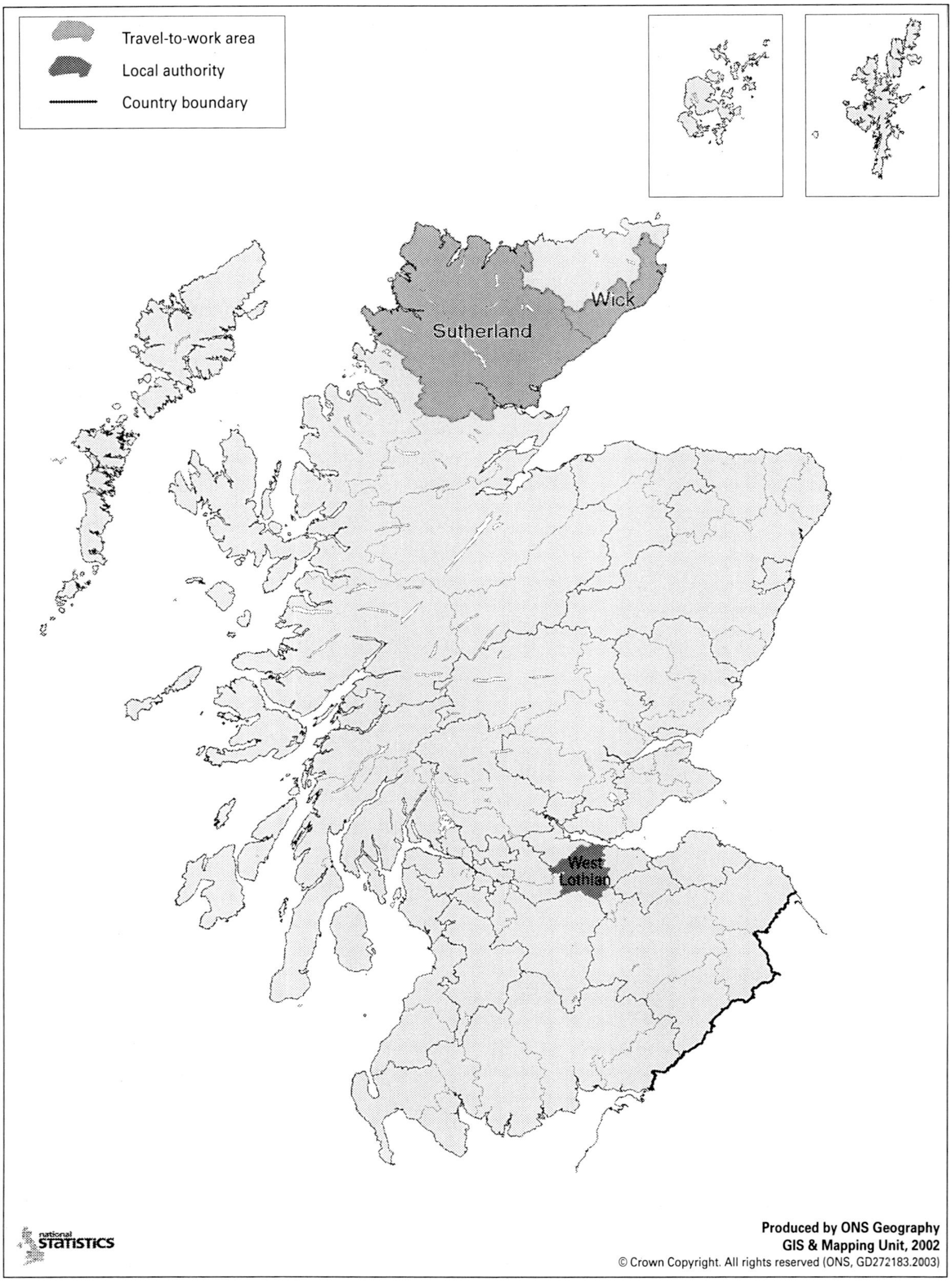

between the country's two largest cities, Glasgow and Edinburgh. Its largest town, Livingston, is only 15 km from Edinburgh, Scotland's rapidly expanding capital. The area is a major centre of manufacturing activity, and has recently experienced job losses as a result of adverse sectoral conditions. West Lothian also has some semi-rural characteristics, with a number of scattered, sparsely populated settlements, relatively isolated from the area's centres of commerce and services, the towns of Livingston and Bathgate, which are well served by Jobcentre facilities. Accordingly, it might be argued that those residing in outlying areas, without ready access to private transport, *may* face somewhat similar barriers to work to job seekers in more remote rural areas.

Finally, it should be noted that local labour market conditions play an important part in providing the context for any research focusing on job seeking.[4] Unemployment rates in Wick and the wider Caithness area have gradually declined from highs registered in the early to mid-1990s, but remain above the Scottish average. Similarly, Sutherland's unemployment has been, and continues to be, well above the national and Highlands averages. It should, however, be noted that seasonal fluctuations have an important impact on the Wick and Sutherland labour markets, which tend to experience sharp increases in unemployment during the winter months, reflecting the decline in tourism employment. West Lothian has witnessed lower unemployment rates in recent years, and although adverse sectoral conditions resulted in substantial job losses during the 2000–03 period, unemployment has (at the time of writing) remained at or below the national average.

Hence, the case studies comprise a centrally located, peri-urban labour market (West Lothian) with unemployment rates generally near the national average, which is to be compared with a remote rural town and a sparsely populated rural labour market (Wick and Sutherland respectively) with unemployment rates generally above the national average, and considerably higher than average depending on seasonal economic impacts. These very different labour markets provide the comparative framework for the research detailed in this report – a framework that will help us to investigate and understand similarities and differences in the experiences of job seekers, and the influence of factors such as remoteness and rurality, the dynamics of local labour market conditions, and the personal and circumstantial barriers to work faced by job seekers (and particularly those at risk of long-term unemployment).

2 Job seeking and the role of ICT: survey findings

This chapter considers the results of the first phase research, and specifically provides: a profile of the sample groups; a discussion of the job search methods used by survey respondents; and an analysis of job seekers' access to, awareness of, and skills relating to ICT. Finally, lessons to be drawn from the survey research are discussed.

Profile of the sample groups

The first phase research involved the amalgamation and interrogation of two existing datasets. Both datasets were developed as a result of commissioned research into employability and job seeking issues. As noted above, 300 responses were gathered in West Lothian, and 190 in Wick and Sutherland. Under the classifications used by the Scottish Executive's *Scottish Household Survey*[5] over one-third (36 per cent) of respondents to the original survey in West Lothian resided in areas classified as 'accessible rural', with a further 30 per cent residing in 'accessible small towns' and 34 per cent in 'urban areas'. Using the same classifications, 85 per cent of those surveyed in the Wick TTWA resided in a 'very remote small town' and a further 15 per cent in 'very remote rural' areas. In Sutherland, 74 per cent of respondents lived in 'very remote rural' areas, with a further 22 per cent in 'remote rural' areas. The remaining 4 per cent of respondents were resident in 'accessible rural' areas, 'remote small towns' or 'other urban' areas. Accordingly, below we are able to discuss the impact of 'rurality' on the take-up and use of ICT, and especially the Internet, as a job search tool.

Substantial minorities in both sample groups were 'long-term unemployed' (using the ILO definition of unemployed and available for work for 12 months or more). As Table 1 illustrates, more than one-third of respondents in the West Lothian sample, and two-fifths (in total) of those from Wick and Sutherland were long-term unemployed, and the majority of both sample groups had been unemployed for at least six months. The West Lothian sample group featured a higher proportion of young people (defined here as the 18–24 age group) than the Wick and Sutherland sample (28 per cent, compared with 20 per cent in both Wick and Sutherland). Respondents interviewed in Wick and Sutherland were, conversely, much more likely to be aged '50 plus' (an age group which, like 18–24 year olds, is specifically targeted by welfare to work initiatives). However, the majority of both sample groups fell into the middle category ('25–49 years'). The average age of respondents in this category was relatively similar across the sample groups (at 35.5 years in West Lothian, 37.0 years in Wick and 38.6 years in Sutherland).

The educational attainment of the sample groups was rather similar, despite the presence of a higher proportion of long-term unemployed people in the Wick and Sutherland cohort. The vast majority of respondents in all areas had fairly limited qualifications – 79 per cent of West Lothian job seekers, 77 per cent of those from Wick and 71 per cent of those from Sutherland were not qualified to Scottish Higher Grade level (the equivalent of National Vocational Qualification Level 3), the level of qualification generally

Table 1 Percentage of sample in study areas unemployed for 6/12 months

Duration	Sutherland	Wick	West Lothian	Combined study areas
6 months +	58	67	55	58
12 months +	37	45	34	37

required for admittance to higher education in Scotland (Table 2). Only around 45 per cent of the general Scottish labour force is similarly unqualified. Clearly, those with few qualifications will be less mobile in terms of their interaction with the labour market, and will be limited in the range and type of employment that they can pursue.

Finally, it should be acknowledged that access to transport and the ability to travel are particularly important in determining the opportunities that job seekers are able to pursue in rural labour markets, and elsewhere. Respondents across all the study areas demonstrated a considerable degree of flexibility with regards to travelling to work. More than half of all job seekers were willing to travel up to 40 km or beyond on a daily basis to work (see Table 3). However, in more remote Wick and Sutherland, job seekers were of necessity much more flexible. In total, two-fifths of these respondents suggested that they would be willing to travel more than 40 km to and from work on a daily basis (35 per cent of Wick job seekers and 51 per cent of those from the Sutherland TTWA). In contrast, only 7 per cent of those residing in the more centrally located West Lothian labour market made the same claim.

These findings appear to reflect the impact of geographical remoteness on job seekers' search strategies. For those living in isolated communities in the northern Scottish Highlands, the number and type of job opportunities available in their immediate area is likely to be severely limited, necessitating extensive travelling in some cases. On the other hand, those West Lothian job seekers who

Table 2 Level of qualification attained by respondents, by study area (%)

Level of qualification	Sutherland	Wick	West Lothian	Combined study areas
None[a]	29	44	37	37
SCE 'Standard' Grade/equivalent[b]	42	33	42	40
SCE 'Higher' Grade/equivalent[c]	14	10	13	13
Higher education qualification[d]	12	9	5	7
Degree/equivalent	4	4	4	4
Total (rounded)	100	100	100	100

a 'None' includes those naming vocational qualifications not recognised in the *Labour Force Survey*.

b 'Standard Grade or equivalent' includes SCE Ordinary and Standard Grades, GSVQ, RSA diploma level and SVQ 1–2.

c 'Higher Grade or equivalent' includes SCE Higher Grades, GSVQ advanced, RSA advanced diploma, SVQ level 3.

d 'Higher Education qualification' includes HND, HNC, SVQ 4 and professional qualifications.

Table 3 Daily travelling distance time considered acceptable by respondents (%)

Acceptable travelling distance each way	Sutherland	Wick	West Lothian	Combined study areas
Immediate area only	8	3	10	8
Up to 15 km	16	32	38	35
Up to 40 km	24	29	45	39
Up to 80 km	27	20	7	11
Over 80 km	24	15	0	7
Total (rounded)	100	100	100	100

stated that they would commute for up to, but not more than, 40 km each day nonetheless included much of the central belt of Scotland (including the country's two largest cities) within their search area. In these circumstances, it is perhaps worrying that approximately one-third of job seekers in Wick and 16 per cent of those in Sutherland would not contemplate travelling beyond 15 km to work. Given the remoteness of some local settlements in these areas (especially in the vast Sutherland TTWA) many of these individuals were effectively limiting their job search to their immediate locality only.

The reasons behind this reluctance to travel are very often all too practical. Levels of private transport ownership were low amongst all sample groups (34 per cent in Wick, 37 per cent in Sutherland and 33 per cent in West Lothian). In all areas the long-term unemployed were also more severely disadvantaged in terms of the availability of private transport (21 per cent in both Wick and Sutherland and 22 per cent in West Lothian). However, whereas a lack of *driving skills* was an important limiting factor in West Lothian, a lack of access and financial constraints appeared to be more problematic in Wick and Sutherland. Less than two-fifths of West Lothian respondents (38 per cent) held a driving licence compared with approximately 75 per cent of those in Wick and 61 per cent of Sutherland job seekers. Yet despite the fact that the majority of these Wick and Sutherland job seekers hold current driving licences, comparatively few had access to their own transport. It would appear that many job seekers hold realistic views about the need to commute, but too often lack the means to make good on a generally flexible approach to 'getting to work'. The practical transport problems and geographical barriers faced by many job seekers (and especially those in rural areas) are likely to limit not only their ability to pursue job opportunities, but also the accessibility of local services. It is in this context that ICT-based services for job seekers have been developed. However, as we will see below, the impact of these services has been marginal for many amongst the unemployed.

Job search methods used by respondents

The job search methods currently used by unemployed people in these very different labour markets should offer some indication as to the relative importance of ICT, informal social networking and more traditional, 'formal' services, and the potential for an expansion in the role of Internet or other ICT-based provision. As noted above, we might hypothesise that those residing in remote rural communities are more likely to rely on alternative methods of job seeking, and less on the formal services that are provided by public agencies. Indeed, our initial findings highlight the different approaches adopted in the more remote Wick and Sutherland labour markets, where Jobcentre facilities are few or non-existent, as opposed to the more centrally located West Lothian. In remote rural areas such as Wick and Sutherland, it would appear that informal methods (ranging from direct approaches to employers to social networking though personal contacts) are a crucial part of day-to-day job seeking activities. In West Lothian, on the other hand, the highly formalised services offered by the Jobcentre Plus agency were more important.

Table 4 illustrates this point. When asked about the job search methods that they used on a weekly basis, West Lothian respondents were far more likely to mention the information facilities and advice of staff in Jobcentres. Almost 70 per cent of West Lothian respondents had received advice from Jobcentre staff on a weekly basis, compared with only 43 per cent of those from Wick and 47 per cent of Sutherland respondents (who had mostly received advice from Jobcentre staff over the telephone). Clearly, the remoteness of some settlements in the northern Highlands makes it impossible for job seekers to travel to the area's 'local' Jobcentre on a regular basis. However, the freephone telephone helplines offered by Jobcentre Plus appear to be unable to replicate the relationship established between job seekers and staff within 'real' Jobcentre settings, at least in terms of numbers of contacts. Conversely, Wick and Sutherland sample members were much more likely to use personal contacts and direct approaches on a regular basis to look for work. Only 42 per cent of West Lothian job seekers (and only 27 per cent of the long-term unemployed) had used their contacts to look for work on a weekly basis, compared with 73 per cent of those in Wick and 74 per cent of Sutherland respondents – figures that were constant even when the sample was analysed by unemployment duration (around a threshold of 12 months of unemployment).

In both study areas, the Internet appears to be an important job search tool for a small – but still significant – group of job seekers, with 16 per cent of Wick and Sutherland respondents and 18 per cent of those in West Lothian using web-based services on a weekly basis. However, in this case the internal geography of the Wick and Sutherland labour markets had an important impact. The figure of 16 per cent using the Internet on a weekly basis masks a wide variation between the town-based Wick TTWA, where Jobcentre facilities are available (9 per cent), and the more remote settlements of Sutherland (28 per cent). Although Sutherland job seekers were generally slightly more highly qualified than their Wick counterparts, a characteristic that may have some impact on Internet access (see below), it would appear that location is important in determining ICT use in remote rural areas.

A closer examination of the methods used by respondents to successfully identify opportunities reveals the still marginal role of the Internet as a job search tool. Table 5 shows a fairly even spread of search methods used by unemployed people to identify 'the last job that they applied for'. Once

Table 4 Respondents using selected job search methods on a weekly basis (%)

Job search method	Sutherland	Wick	West Lothian	Combined study areas
Newspaper advertisements	94	96	92	94
Jobcentre notice boards	31	59	77	66
Advice from Jobcentre staff	47	43	69	60
Personal contacts	73	74	42	54
Direct approach	51	68	25	39
Internet	28	9	18	18

Table 5 Job search methods used to identify most recently pursued job opportunity (%)

Job search method	Sutherland	Wick	West Lothian	Combined study areas
Personal contacts/direct	50	37	28	33
Jobcentre notice boards	4	22	32	25
Newspaper advertisements	23	20	17	18
Advice from Jobcentre staff	9	16	11	12
Other	4	2	9	7
Community bodies/facilities	9	2	4	4
Internet	1	1	0	1
Total (rounded)	100	100	100	100

again, formal Jobcentre services appear more important in the centrally located West Lothian labour market, with informal methods playing a greater role in Wick and Sutherland. Once again, within the Wick and Sutherland labour markets, differences in job seeker behaviour between the two TTWAs were apparent. The more remote Sutherland job seekers were more likely to have relied on informal methods (50 per cent compared with 37 per cent of Wick TTWA respondents), while those from the Wick TTWA were much more likely to have used Jobcentre staff (16 per cent compared with 9 per cent) and information facilities (22 per cent compared with 4 per cent) to identify their most recent job opportunity.

Perhaps more importantly, although job seeking via the Internet appeared to be a regular activity for almost one-fifth of job seekers, very few had recently found success in identifying an appropriate vacancy on-line. Only two respondents (1 per cent of the sample) from Wick and Sutherland had accessed Internet job search sites to identify a recent vacancy. None of the West Lothian-based respondents had used the Internet to identify their most recently pursued job. For many of these unemployed people, the Internet remained of little value in their job search.

Job seekers and ICT: access, skills and awareness

If facilities delivered via the Internet are to enable job seekers to identify appropriate vacancies, and provide opportunities to extend social networks, *access* to ICT is an issue of central importance. Comparing domestic access to ICT across our study areas, members of the West Lothian sample emerged as slightly more likely to have a home or mobile telephone, at 83 per cent, compared with 76 per cent in Wick and Sutherland. As Table 6 shows, West Lothian job seekers were also more likely to have a PC with private Internet connection (26 per cent compared with 19 per cent in the combined Wick and Sutherland areas). However, members of the Wick and Sutherland sample who resided in the more rural Sutherland TTWA were clearly more likely to have Internet access (27 per cent, compared with 12 per cent of those in the Wick TTWA). They were also more likely to have a home telephone (85 per cent, compared with 68 per cent in Wick).

It is perhaps more worrying that a significant minority (15 per cent) of those from rural Sutherland reported that they did not have a home or mobile telephone. (Among the long-term unemployed this rose to 21 per cent.) Although research with unemployed job seekers elsewhere has shown up to 25 per cent not having access to a telephone,[6] the above findings are particularly important given the geographical and policy context. The telephone-based services provided by Jobcentre Plus to clients in very remote areas of Sutherland supposedly deliver high quality advice and information to those unable to attend Jobcentre offices in person. Yet there remains a minority of Sutherland clients without ready access to a telephone, who are required to 'phone in' from others' residences or public telephone kiosks, in order to access the agency's services.

While area-based factors may account for some of the differences in ICT access and usage, it is likely that other, personal barriers will have limited

Table 6 Home access to ICT, by study area (%)

Form of access	Sutherland	Wick	West Lothian	Combined study areas
Internet	27	12	26	23
Telephone	85	68	83	80

the ability of some job seekers to take up ICT-based services. Long-term unemployed people in *all* areas were rather less likely to have Internet or telephone access at home. It would appear that this in turn reflects a combination of financial and skills barriers faced by the more disadvantaged. Whereas only 15 per cent of those job seekers reporting a total household income of less than £150 per week (then approximately €236) had access to the Internet at home, the figure for all other respondents was 43 per cent. Similarly, only 15 per cent of those in the lower income bracket used the Internet to look for work on a weekly basis, compared with 27 per cent of those with a weekly income above £150.

Those with limited skills were similarly disadvantaged in terms of accessing the Internet. As Table 7 shows, those qualified to the general level of 'SCE Higher Grade or equivalent' were more than three times more likely to have home Internet access than those with no qualifications (37 per cent, compared with 12 per cent). Higher qualified job seekers were also much more likely to use the Internet to look for work on a weekly basis (34 per cent, compared with 8 per cent of those not similarly qualified).

Another considerable concern for policy makers must lie in the admission of many job seekers, across *all* income and skill groups, that they lack confidence in using even basic forms of ICT. When asked to rate their own attainment across a range of areas, the vast majority of respondents described their skills as 'good or adequate'. Yet it is notable that while less than 10 per cent of all respondents considered their occupational skills, literacy, numeracy or communication skills to be 'poor', 58 per cent held similarly negative views about their ICT skills.

Clearly, self-reporting of skill levels may not reflect an objective analysis of the individual's actual attainment. For example, both Scottish and UK-level research suggests that approximately one-fifth of *all* people of working age have poor basic document literacy (i.e. reading) skills – at a level 'below the standard norm expected of an 11 year old' (DfEE, 1999; Scottish Executive, 2001a). If there are large numbers amongst the general adult population with low literacy skills, we might reasonably hypothesise that these problems are likely to be more severe amongst the unemployed and low-skilled – a reality not reflected in respondents' assessments of their own literacy skills. However, given that it is common for job seekers to demonstrate a degree of over-confidence in evaluating their skills attainment – perhaps reflecting the rhetoric used by many on a day-to-day basis when attempting to 'sell' themselves to employers – the fact that job seekers were so clear about their *lack of skills* with regards to ICT may reflect particularly severe problems in this area.

Educational attainment would again appear to be closely linked to job seekers' perceptions here. Those qualified to the general level of 'SCE Higher Grade or equivalent' were much less likely to consider their ICT skills to be poor (36 per cent, compared with 78 per cent of those with no

Table 7 Respondents with home Internet access and using the Internet to look for work on a weekly basis, by educational attainment (%)

Respondents' general educational attainment	Percentage with Internet access	Percentage using Internet weekly
None	12	8
SVQ 1–2/SCE O Grade or equivalent	25	16
At least SVQ 3/SCE H Grade or equivalent	37	34
All respondents	23	18

qualifications and 55 per cent of those with intermediate qualifications). Younger job seekers, who tend to hold more formal qualifications, were also generally more confident about using ICT: only 49 per cent of 18–24 year olds described their ICT skills as poor, compared with 75 per cent of those aged over 50, and 57 per cent of other job seekers. This is particularly noteworthy given that 18–24 year olds were only slightly more likely than the '50 plus' age group to have home Internet access (although both groups were below-average in terms of regularly using Internet to look for work, at 14 per cent and 12 per cent respectively).

Age, attitudes towards ICT, perceived and real gaps in technical skills, and perhaps most importantly educational attainment and income status may all impact on the ability and willingness of job seekers to use new forms of technology as a means of looking for work. However, there is a clear need to 'unpack' these variables, and the relationships between them. For example, those with lower household incomes are both more likely to be long-term unemployed and less likely to have access to the Internet at home. Yet, thus far, it is unclear as to whether the digital divide experienced by many of these individuals is a symptom of their long-term unemployment (in itself linked to lower educational attainment), their income status, or a combination of these and other factors.

In order to test the association between individual and labour market characteristics and ICT access and use, a binary logistic regression model was used (see Box 2). The model examined the association between two dependent variables (home Internet access; weekly use of the Internet for job seeking) and selected job seeker and area characteristics that emerged as potentially relevant from the above analysis. Dummy variables for the 'West Lothian' study area and the 'Sutherland' TTWA (as opposed to the broader 'Wick and Sutherland' area) were used. Before the regression model was developed, a correlation matrix of all potential variables was applied and variables that exhibited statistically significant correlations were removed.

Box 2: Binary logistic regression model

Logistic regression is a statistical method used to measure the relationship between a categorical, dependent variable (i.e. the variable whose behaviour or change we wish to measure) and a set of one or more predictor or independent variables (the factors whose effects on the dependent variable we wish to observe). A binary logistic regression model can be used when the dependent variable is dichotomous (e.g. an answer of either 'yes' or 'no'), as in this case: where we are attempting to predict which respondents were either likely to have/or not have home Internet access (in the first equation); and which respondents either used/or did not use the Internet as a job search tool (in the second equation). The model enables us to group people with respect to their predicted action. In terms of results, a positive 'regression coefficient' indicates a positive association between the independent and dependent variables (as in Table 8, where, for example, being in a higher income group is positively related to them having Internet access). If this value is negative, then there is a negative association between the independent and dependent variables (as in Table 8, where being aged 18–24 was negatively associated with Internet access – i.e. those in this age group were less likely to have access to the Internet at home). The significance levels given for each independent variable indicate whether that particular independent variable is a statistically significant predictor of the dependent variable. If the significance is <0.05 (i.e. 5 per cent) then the result is generally considered to be statistically significant. This means that there is only a 5 per cent probability that the observed result is due to chance, rather than there being the result of a 'real' association between the variables in question.

As Table 8 illustrates, the strong association between job seekers' skills and ICT access is confirmed. Both formal qualifications and job seekers' perceived ICT skills appear to be significantly associated with Internet access (with those perceiving their skills to be 'good or adequate' more likely to have on-line facilities at home). Home Internet access was also associated with income status, reflecting the manner in which those with higher household incomes (often reflecting the presence of a working partner) are better able to cope with the costs of hardware purchase and connection charges. Although there was a positive association between Internet access and residence in both West Lothian and Sutherland, the degree of significance was stronger for the latter.

The statistically significant association between factors such as gender and income status and Internet access was not replicated when Internet job seeking was analysed. There was, however, a strong association between measures of respondents' skills (formal qualifications and perceptions of ICT skills) and their use of the Internet as a job search tool. While residence in West Lothian was not strongly associated with web-based job seeking, there was a significant positive relationship between Sutherland residence and the use of the Internet. Internet access and use therefore appears to be associated with a combination of factors related to skills and qualifications, income and gender. Perhaps more importantly, these findings confirm that those in more remote areas (such as the isolated settlements of Sutherland) are more likely to invest in domestic ICT facilities and use the Internet to look for work. In these areas, more so than peri-urban labour markets, there may be an awareness that the weakness of formal service infrastructures necessitates the adoption of 'alternative' job search strategies and approaches to social networking,

Table 8 Respondents with home Internet access and using the Internet to look for work on a weekly basis, by selected individual characteristics

	Home Internet access		Weekly Internet use	
Respondents' characteristics	**Beta**	**Significance**	**Beta**	**Significance**
Level of qualification	0.270	0.054*	0.438	0.002***
Perception of ICT skills	1.340	0.000***	1.167	0.000***
Income group	0.484	0.000***	0.148	0.126
Resident in West Lothian[a]	1.257	0.006***	0.517	0.281
Resident in Sutherland[a]	1.925	0.000***	1.389	0.011**
Unemployment duration	–0.607	0.074*	–0.731	0.049**
Age 18–24	–1.193	0.004***	–0.897	0.039**
Male	–0.943	0.012**	–0.149	0.689
Have children under 18	–0.570	0.108	–0.281	0.455
Constant	–4.170	0.000***	–3.919	0.000***

Beta co-efficients estimated from binary logistic regression

*** $p<0.01$ (1% level of significance); ** $p<0.05$ (5% level of significance); * $p<0.1$ (10% level of significance)
[a] Base area is Wick TTWA

with web-based activities offering one potential source of information and communication. However, it should be noted throughout that ICT-based job seeking remains the activity of a minority. For most unemployed people, across a range of skill groups and social classes, technology-based forms of job seeking and social interaction remain a somewhat obscure concept.

Lessons from the survey research: ICT, job seeking and the digital divide

The above findings demonstrate that job seekers' access to and use of ICT is affected by a range of factors related to individual characteristics, personal circumstances, labour market geography and the accessibility of local services. Those living in areas served by Jobcentre facilities appeared to be less likely to rely on informal social networks as a means of identifying job opportunities, and less likely to have used the Internet as a regular job search tool. However, it is also clear that even amongst job seekers, there is a digital divide. Access and use of the Internet was more common amongst job seekers at the 'top end' of the scale in terms of educational attainment, income group and (self-assessed) ICT skills. Furthermore, and perhaps most worryingly of all, young people and the long-term unemployed (exactly the client groups that can most struggle to access informal, social networks in the labour market) were disadvantaged in terms of ICT access and use (although, as noted above, young people were more likely to perceive themselves as having adequate skills to use ICT).

The geography of local labour markets, *in combination with the accessibility of services for job seekers*, also appeared to have an important impact. Respondents in the remote rural Sutherland TTWA were much more likely to acknowledge the potential benefits of ICT as a job search tool. Yet job seekers in the remote rural town of Wick were far less likely to have used ICT to look for work (even less so than their counterparts in the centrally located, peri-urban West Lothian labour market). It would seem that the combination of geographical remoteness and the absence of services on the ground in Sutherland's remote communities has led to the growth of Internet use as a means of job seeking.

These findings suggest that the government's move towards ICT-based services may be welcomed by some job seekers, especially in remote rural areas. ICT-based services have the capacity to enable recipients to develop new skills, access information on employment and training, extend their social networks and communicate their needs to service providers and policy makers more effectively. Given the particular importance of social networking in rural labour markets, and the Internet's potential value in extending network relations, as well as providing 'official' information, an expansion and further development of services delivered through ICT may offer considerable benefits. In terms of the development of formal information services, any measures that improve the accessibility of information about job and training opportunities, as well as (crucially) the availability of community transport, may have positive impacts in rural areas.

However, if these services are to be effective, action is required to address the digital divide experienced by many amongst the most disadvantaged unemployed people. Without a strong support infrastructure, the expansion of ICT-based provision (if used to replace 'real', on-the-ground services) may in fact deepen the sense of exclusion experienced by these job seekers. Furthermore, our findings highlight the reality that, even in remote rural areas, ICT-based job seeking remains of marginal importance. Some of the reasons for the marginal use of ICT were considered in the focus groups discussed below. It may be that the development of more flexible and interactive official websites will be required if more job seekers are to be drawn towards using the

Internet as a job search tool. Internet-based services that facilitate informal networking and social interaction, as well as formally advertising vacancies, and that allow job seekers and employers to communicate more openly, may have a greater role to play in the future provision of services for job seekers in rural labour markets.

3 Attitudes to ICT-based job seeking: focus group findings

This chapter considers the results of the second phase of the research. It first presents a profile of the focus groups and discusses the context for individuals' contributions, in terms of the access, skills and awareness of ICT amongst focus group participants. It then discusses focus group participants' attitudes towards ICT-based job seeking, with reference to new technology in Jobcentres, the Internet and telephone helpline services. The search methods predominantly deployed by unemployed people in the two study areas are then discussed, along with the impact of informal networking and local labour market conditions on job seeking. Finally, the chapter briefly discusses lessons to be drawn from the focus group research.

Profile of the focus groups

A total of 12 focus groups were conducted, involving 72 participants across West Lothian, Wick and Sutherland. Focus group participants were contacted via community-based service providers or through direct approaches made by members of the research team at Jobcentres. Group meetings were held at locations familiar to participants, often community centres or local training facilities, which job seekers were already attending on a regular basis. The one exception involved a telephone conference call focus group held between five participants scattered across more remote areas of Sutherland. This group brought together, for example, one participant residing in Lochinver, on Sutherland's west coast and others at Bonar Bridge in east-central Sutherland, some 80 km away by road, and Helmsdale, on the east coast, 130 km away. This focus group, which in itself might be seen as effectively harnessing ICT to gather together job seekers located in small, remote communities, proved highly useful – importantly, job seekers had been briefed on an individual basis as to the format and focus of the group discussion. These job seekers were approached through a Wick-based public sector intermediary, from whom they had already received 'remote' job search counselling and advice services by telephone. An audio-conferencing package was used (provided by BT) to ensure that a high quality recording of the telephone-based focus group was available to the research team. All other focus groups were also recorded.

In West Lothian, specific client groups were targeted. Accordingly, separate focus groups were held with long-term unemployed people (duration over 12 months) aged 25 and over, contacted through a New Deal training provider; young people (aged 16–24), contacted through New Deal Gateway and youth training intermediaries; job seekers aged 50 and over, contacted through a community-level job search service provider; and 'women returners' (female job seekers with young children), contacted through a local family centre providing both training and childcare support. These clients were targeted so as to provide an insight into potential barriers to ICT-based job seeking (and other job search activities) faced by groups who *can* particularly struggle to gain access to work, due to skills gaps and a lack of recent and relevant work experience, age-based barriers or family and caring responsibilities. While focus groups held in Wick and Sutherland were designed to draw a more 'general' membership, reflecting the limited pool of potential participants, three groups were composed entirely of long-term unemployed people aged 25 and over. The remaining three groups were mixed in terms of the age, gender and unemployment duration of participants. Table 9 provides further detail on focus group membership and locations.

Table 9 Location and membership of focus groups

Study area	Focus group location	Membership (duration)	Number of participants
West Lothian	Broxburn Family and Community Centre, Broxburn	Women returners (various durations)	5
West Lothian	'The Workplace' support centre, Whitburn	Aged 50 and over (various durations)	7
West Lothian	New Deal Gateway Course, Livingston	Young people (at least 6 months)	10
West Lothian	New Deal/Skillseekers (youth training) Courses, Livingston	Young people (various durations)	7
West Lothian	New Deal 25+ Intensive Activity Programme, Livingston	LTU adults (at least 12 months)	9
West Lothian	New Deal 25+ Intensive Activity Programme, Livingston	LTU adults (at least 12 months)	5
Wick	Jobcentre Plus Programme Centre, North Highland College, Wick	LTU adults (at least 12 months)	6
Wick	Jobcentre Plus Programme Centre North Highland College, Wick	LTU adults (at least 12 months)	5
Wick	Jobcentre Plus Programme Centre North Highland College, Wick	Mixed (various durations)	3
Sutherland	Community centre, Lairg	Mixed (various durations)	6
Sutherland	Community centre, Brora	Mixed (various durations)	4
Sutherland	Sutherland Conference Call: participants in Bonar Bridge (2), Brora, Helmsdale, Lochinver	LTU adults (at least 12 months)	5

Focus group participants and ICT: access, skills and awareness

Before discussing job seekers' views of ICT-based job seeking in detail, it is perhaps worth examining the context on which individuals based their comments – i.e. their experience of and access to ICT and the Internet. Of the 72 job seekers who participated in focus groups, 70 completed short questionnaires, which gathered details about their knowledge of ICT and the Internet, their perceived level of ICT skills and their use of new technologies in job seeking. Although not necessarily statistically representative of the full client population, these discussions provide many useful insights. As Table 10 illustrates, members of our Sutherland focus groups were clearly more likely to have access to the Internet at home. Whereas four-fifths of these job seekers were on-line at home, the figure was less than one-third for West Lothian participants, and just over one-fifth for those residing in the Wick TTWA.

Fairly high proportions amongst our focus group participants in both Sutherland and West Lothian had used the Internet *at some time*, although this was much less the case for Wick job seekers. However, perhaps the clearest finding emerging from Table 10 is that even amongst those with access to the Internet at home, this form of ICT was considered somewhat marginal to their job search activities (a similar conclusion to that reached following our quantitative analysis of

Table 10 Focus group participants' access to and use of ICT (number of responses)

Characteristics of participants	No. of focus group participants by area Sutherland	Wick	West Lothian
Internet access at home	12	3	12
Telephone access at home	15	9	36
Used Internet weekly	9	3	12
Used Internet at some time	2	2	16
Never used Internet	4	9	13
Used Internet for job search weekly	6	0	6
Used Internet for job search at some time	2	4	15
Never used Internet for job search	7	10	20
Considered ICT skills 'good'	6	4	4
Considered ICT skills 'adequate'	4	4	25
Considered ICT skills 'poor'	5	6	12
Total no. of focus group participants	15	14	41

survey responses). Of the 70 participants across all three study areas who provided questionnaire responses, 27 had access to the Internet at home and 24 used it on a regular (i.e. weekly) basis. Yet only 12 used the Internet on a regular basis to look for work. Over half of those attending Sutherland and West Lothian focus groups had used the Internet at some time for job seeking, although in the latter study area this figure almost certainly reflects the limited job search training provided as an element of New Deal options.

Table 11 provides further information on home Internet access amongst focus group participants. It is clear that male focus group participants were much more likely to have access to the Internet at home (although it should be noted that a relatively small proportion of all participants were women). While those aged 50 and over were again more likely to have access to the Internet than job seekers aged 18–24, both groups at the extremes of age range lagged behind the 25–49 year-olds, more than half of whom were on-line at home. Table 11 also shows that focus group participants qualified to SCE Higher Grade/A Level or above were clearly more likely to have home Internet access – nearly twice as likely as those without qualifications. Indeed, educational attainment appeared to be a better indicator of Internet access amongst focus group participants than unemployment duration. Similar proportions of long-term and short-term job seekers had access to the Internet, with long-term unemployed people actually slightly more likely to be on-line at home. Finally, those who considered themselves to have 'good' ICT skills were also rather more likely than others to have access to the Internet.

Table 12 again illustrates the somewhat marginal status of ICT-based job seeking amongst our focus group participants. Although more than one-third of Sutherland focus group participants used the Internet every week to look for work, this represented the equivalent of only half of those who had access to the Internet at home in that area. None of our Wick focus group participants used the Internet on a weekly basis to look for work, along with only a small minority of West Lothian-based job seekers (6 of a total of 41 participants who provided questionnaire responses in that area). While just over half of all men with Internet access used the web to look for work on a weekly basis, none of the four women who attended our focus groups and were on-line at home used the Internet as a job search tool.

Table 11 Focus group participants with home Internet access by participant characteristic (number of responses)

Characteristics of participants	No. of participants with Internet access	Total no. of participants
Sutherland resident	12	15
Wick resident	3	14
West Lothian resident	12	41
Male	23	55
Female	4	15
Aged 16–24	5	21
Aged 25–49	15	29
Aged 50+	7	20
Qualified to SCE H Grade/above	9	15
Qualified to SCE Standard Grade/equivalent	10	28
No qualifications	8	27
Considered ICT skills 'good'	12	14
Considered ICT skills 'adequate'	11	33
Considered ICT skills 'poor'	4	23
Long-term unemployed	15	37
Not long-term unemployed	12	33

Table 12 Focus group participants using the Internet on a weekly basis to look for work by participant characteristic (number of responses)

Characteristics of participants	No. of participants Internet job seeking	Total no. of participants
Sutherland resident	6	15
Wick resident	0	14
West Lothian resident	6	41
Male	12	55
Female	0	15
Aged 16–24	1	21
Aged 25–49	8	29
Aged 50+	3	20
Qualified to SCE H Grade/above	5	15
Qualified to SCE Standard Grade/equivalent	5	28
No qualifications	2	27
Considered ICT skills 'good'	4	14
Considered ICT skills 'adequate'	8	33
Considered ICT skills 'poor'	0	23
Long-term unemployed	8	37
Not long-term unemployed	4	33
Has home Internet access	8	27
No home Internet access	4	43

In summary, job seekers' use of the Internet as a job search tool to some extent mirrored the findings for ICT access. Focus group participants at the extremes of the working population age range, the unqualified, and those considering their own ICT skills to be less than 'adequate' emerged as least likely to use the Internet as a job search tool. However, as we have seen, although those with home Internet access were much more likely than others to look for work via the world-wide-web, *regular* Internet job seeking was a minority activity amongst all focus group participants.

Accordingly, our focus group discussions sought to clarify why Internet job seeking was not more important amongst the unemployed, with reference to the issues of access, skills and awareness. The discussion within groups also focused on the impact of the accessibility and availability of local services and labour market conditions on perceptions of the Internet and other ICT-based solutions. Our findings highlight the need for 'virtual' job search provision to be linked with local services 'in real life', and to reflect the complexities of the recruitment and job search process in local labour markets, particularly in rural areas.

Focus group participants' attitudes towards ICT-based job seeking

Attitudes towards new technology at Jobcentres

In general terms, job seekers in West Lothian believed that the introduction of jobpoints had had a positive impact on the services provided by Jobcentre Plus. The traditional 'cards and boards' system, which jobpoints replaced, was far less popular. Job seekers complained that the information provided on job cards was very often outdated, with a number of focus group participants remembering occasions when they had enquired about opportunities advertised on cards only to find that the vacancy had been filled some days before. In contrast, the vast majority of those who had used jobpoints perceived the information available to be up to date and relevant. A small minority noted that the old problem of outdated and insufficient information remained, with one job seeker (from the '50+' West Lothian focus group) arguing that the jobpoint system was generally effective but required better 'housekeeping'.

Almost all focus group participants who had used jobpoints considered them to be user-friendly. Interestingly, there seemed to be little difference in job seekers' attitudes on the basis of age. Members of the '50+' focus group and other older job seekers appeared to be largely in favour of the new technology. Although initially apprehensive, these older job seekers had come to value, in particular, the sense of personal autonomy provided by job points, welcoming an end to the practice of crowding around boards and straining to see past other job seekers. Similar attitudes were also held by members of our focus groups with young people. As one West Lothian job seeker noted:

> *The jobpoints are actually better, because with the cards it was too crowded and people would get in your way. The old way, I used to get really claustrophobic and it never gave you any privacy.*
> (Laura, 18, unemployed six months, West Lothian)

Few focus group participants reported major problems in using the new technology, although some raised the concern that others may have struggled to make the transition to the new system. It was also suggested that additional support should have been provided during the initial period following the introduction of jobpoints.

> *I get on with it fine. But you've got to be shown how to use it. Not everyone will walk in and know how to use the screens, and when they changed it, they changed over night. There was no help for people who didn't know what they were doing.*
> (Frank, 25, unemployed one year, West Lothian)

This view was challenged by other job seekers, however, who commended Jobcentre Plus staff for the support and advice provided during the transition period.

> *They* [jobpoints] *can make a big difference if you know how to work them. It took me a couple of hours to get an idea of how to use them, but I can do it now and they* [Jobcentre staff] *gave me help ...* (Patrick, 37, unemployed five weeks, Wick)

A substantial minority of respondents (across all areas and client groups) complained that jobpoints were regularly to be found out of order, apparently as a result of 'network problems'. This claim was again disputed by the majority, however. It would appear that those using Jobcentres on a regular (e.g. daily) basis were less likely to stress the technical problems, which they agreed *occasionally* affected the system. Nevertheless, some focus group participants strongly argued for a return to the cards and boards system, if only as a back up to the computerised jobpoints.

> *I think that they should go back to the old card system or at least incorporate that system with the computers. Then if the computers were down, you could still do something.* (Peter, 53, unemployed two years, Wick)

In reality, such an approach would be unlikely to be effective, as the full details of vacancy and contact information would still be held on a database accessed by Jobcentre staff, which would not be operational following any network failure that had disabled jobpoints. Indeed, the continued reliance of job seekers on Jobcentre staff to provide the detail of vacancy information, despite the introduction of jobpoints, was identified as a failing of the system by a number of unemployed job seekers, who suggested that the new system had done little to empower Jobcentre clients to conduct their own searches.

> *The terminal gives you a slip. You take the slip to the staff. You ask about the job, they tell you about it. Not very interactive is it?* (Alan, 51, unemployed six months, West Lothian)

However, the main criticism of jobpoints tended to come from those who found that the system over-complicated the process of conducting general, broad-based job searches. A substantial minority of focus group participants in all areas, mostly male job seekers looking for manual work, complained that the design of the jobpoint software, which requires users to specify a sector, occupation and geographical area, was flawed. For those seeking manual labouring or 'general' work, looser categories facilitating a broader job search would have been much more helpful.

> *Since they've computerised the Jobcentre with these things in the middle of the floor – you go in and you have to press a button for local jobs, press a button for the type of job you're looking for, press a button for the area. Me personally, I preferred the old card system, because I haven't got a clue what I'm looking for, and I used to walk in and look at things and think, 'I'll try that'. Now, you've got to have a specific idea. I mean, I'm a manual labourer; I don't have a specific idea.* (Peter, 53, unemployed two years, Wick)

Similar views were expressed by other manual workers. Although these individuals were comfortable using the jobpoint technology, many recalled the one benefit of the old 'cards and boards' approach – that job seekers could skim across a large number of broadly similar opportunities very quickly, comparing pay and conditions between vacancies. This convenience was lost with the introduction of jobpoints, which had in fact slowed the search process for these job seekers.

Many focus group participants in Wick (and the one Sutherland-based respondent who regularly attended the Jobcentre in person) shared the view that jobpoints had over-complicated the job search process. From the perspective of job seekers in these small labour markets, computerised terminals were unnecessary, given the limited number of opportunities available. For these job seekers, the provision of a searchable database holding national and international- level vacancy information did not disguise the obvious lack of *local* opportunities. The consensus appeared to be that jobpoints provided a useful source of highly detailed information for those seeking to leave the area in pursuit of job opportunities. For those remaining, a system offering a general bulletin on the few vacancies that arise on a daily or weekly basis in the local labour market would have been more useful.

> *There are very few local jobs on the job points. I've got a kid, and I'm no wanting to leave the area. There's nothing for me on them. The sort of jobs I'm looking for, it always comes up saying 'sorry, not available'. I've never seen a decent job in Wick on it yet.*
> (Martin, 30, unemployed 15 months, Wick)

> *In my view it's all cosmetic, and it's not through their particular fault. It's just about what jobs are available.*
> (David, 51, unemployed one year, Wick)

> *Hi-tech is fine if it works, but if it doesn't work, it's a waste of money. I think that they've become over-reliant on technology and they're putting too much emphasis on it. That's not using it in the right way.*
> (Iain, 63, unemployed two years, Wick)

In summary, there was a degree of goodwill towards the introduction of jobpoints. However, many job seekers, and especially those who perceived there to be few opportunities in the local labour market, doubted the extent to which the new technology would assist them in finding work. Irrespective of age and area, most job seekers had adapted well to the introduction of jobpoints, in many cases with the assistance of Jobcentre staff. There also appear to be benefits in terms of the privacy and autonomy afforded to job seekers who are no longer forced to gather around displays that were little more than 'lists of jobs pinned to a wall'. Yet our focus group participants, while largely welcoming the arrival of the new system, remained sceptical as to its real value. Furthermore, for those seeking lower skilled general or manual jobs (a substantial proportion of the Jobcentre Plus client group) there were clear drawbacks – the jobpoint system makes searching across a range of general vacancies more difficult, and arguably discourages the broadening of low-skilled workers' job search strategies. For those seeking to search across the limited range of *all* vacancies in small, isolated rural areas, there were similar problems. An important lesson for the (re-)design of ICT-based job search tools would therefore appear to relate to the need to take account of the interaction between local vacancy characteristics and labour market conditions and clients' existing job seeking activities. Changes to the system, enabling a broad-based approach to looking for work may help to address these problems. Generating sufficient appropriate job opportunities for remote rural areas will prove to be a much more difficult task, beyond the scope of the public employment service.

The Internet and job seeking

As noted above, for the majority of focus group participants in all study areas, the Internet played a relatively marginal role in job seeking activities. Both awareness and use of the Internet amongst West Lothian job seekers were fairly low. Those who had used the Internet to look for work at some time had mainly done so as part of a training scheme option (this was particularly the case for members of the New Deal 18-24 and New Deal 25+ client groups). As we have seen, age differences were less obvious than might have been expected. While young people attending focus groups tended to rate their ICT skills as 'good' more often than older job seekers, they were not more likely to use the Internet to look for work. Indeed, although all groups expressed doubts as to the added value provided by the Internet, a number of 'over 50' participants who had used the Jobcentre Plus website remarked on the convenience and privacy offered by web-based services. For others, however, predictable skill barriers seemed insurmountable.

I'm in my sixties and I know nothing about the new technology. To try to learn about that technology now is way beyond my comprehension. A computer sitting in the corner that's blank would stay blank as far as I'm concerned. Every job in my working life has been a manual job, I couldn't work computers.
(Dennis, 65, unemployed one year, West Lothian)

Poor ICT skills were not rare amongst older job seekers, but there was a general willingness to consider learning about the Internet, and an apparent acceptance that 'you have to know about computers'. Yet even amongst those who had access to and regularly used the Internet, awareness of the Jobcentre Plus website and the Internet's broader potential as a job search tool was fairly low – for example, whereas four out of five members of the West Lothian 'women returners' focus group were on-line at home, none had used the Internet to look for work.

Amongst the minority who had used the Internet for job seeking, the Jobcentre Plus website was most often cited as a main information source. There was a consensus amongst Internet-using job seekers in all the study areas that the Jobcentre Plus service was user-friendly, easily navigable and 'fast'. However, a small number of job seekers complained that the site should be more interactive. For these individuals, who tended to have considerable experience in using the Internet, the Jobcentre Plus service compared poorly with some private employment agencies' websites, which enabled users to submit CVs, save search profiles and tailor their job search more effectively.

A more basic complaint was that the description of job opportunities provided by the Jobcentre Plus site was not detailed enough to enable users to make an informed choice, with information on pay and conditions, hours, shift patterns and specific location often missing. It was suggested that the absence of basic information from some vacancy notices was a negative feature that the web-based system shared with the Jobcentre's traditional 'cards and boards' approach. It should be noted, however, that employers, rather than Jobcentre Plus staff, were more often held responsible by job seekers for these problems.

It doesn't matter about the system. It's the same people doing the advertising whatever it is, so you get exactly the same problems – either the information is wrong or information about pay and hours is just not there.
(Phil, 55, unemployed two years, West Lothian)

For West Lothian job seekers, the proximity of Jobcentre Plus facilities made Internet job seeking a supplementary, and in the event somewhat marginal, activity. Perhaps understandably, there was much stronger awareness of the Internet in rural Sutherland, where focus group participants rarely visited the Jobcentre at Wick. As noted above, regular use of the Internet to look for work was rather more common amongst Sutherland-based job seekers attending our focus groups. As with the other focus groups, there was a generally high level of awareness of the Jobcentre Plus website, which was commended by almost all of its users as being user-friendly and easily navigable. However, a familiar concern related to the capacity of ICT-based systems to over-complicate the job search process. A number of focus group participants noted that the small labour pool in Sutherland meant that a searchable database was not required in order to identify local opportunities. It was suggested that the design of the Jobcentre Plus website, which like the jobpoint system requires job seekers to specify area, sector and occupation, was more appropriate for large-scale urban labour markets than remote rural communities, where a simple listing of new vacancies would be more helpful.

I've used the Jobcentre website, but the problem with that is that you're asked for a specific area – construction, sales, whatever – then a job type, then an actual job. You can set up a profile for yourself, but

up here you'd have to set up that many...you can't get just a list of jobs within a 50 mile radius of where you live.
(Rod, 36, unemployed six months, Lairg, Sutherland)

When you search by job what you seem to get is every clerical job in the Highlands or every construction job in the Highlands. What I really want to know is jobs in Lochinver – I'm interested in any jobs that come up. It would be nice if you could just get a list of every vacancy in your area, but it seems impossible.
(George, 54, unemployed two years, Lochinver, Sutherland)

They've got it set up for big urban areas, where you need categories of jobs, but up here there's no need for it. You could fit a list of local jobs on half a page.
(John, 34, unemployed one year, Lairg, Sutherland)

With the Internet you have to type in a type of job and where you live, but it gives you a list of jobs across a huge area, and you have to go through a long list of categories. If you lived in the city, I'm sure it'd be great, but up here it's not.
(Eric, 26, unemployed five months, Brora, Sutherland)

Again, even those using the Internet regularly to look for work were sceptical about its potential for improving their job prospects. For these job seekers, the main benefits of the Internet were related to convenience or cost – for example, accessing on-line versions of local newspapers was considered cheaper than buying hard copies. Members of our Wick-based focus groups who used the Internet to look for work were similarly sceptical about its value, and job seekers in this area (which has its own Jobcentre) were generally less likely to have used the Internet as a job search tool in the first place. There was a common perception that Internet job seeking could add little to the more easily accessible services provided by the local Jobcentre.

The general consensus among job seekers in areas served by local Jobcentre facilities was that there was little need for additional Internet services. Awareness and use was generally rather limited in West Lothian, while in the remote rural town of Wick, focus group participants viewed web-based job seeking as offering a useful alternative for those seeking to leave the area, but providing little added value to the services already available for those looking for work locally. Sutherland-based focus group participants were more likely to use the Internet as a regular job search tool, reflecting the absence of formal services in the area's remote rural communities. Yet even for these job seekers, Internet services were useful only as a means of identifying opportunities outwith the local area, or as a cheaper and more convenient way of accessing already-available newspaper advertisements. Most of these job seekers could see little point in using the Jobcentre Plus website to access vacancy information available through the same agency's telephone helpline facility. There is some evidence that a more targeted website, designed to provide easily accessible 'local jobs lists', may attract more rural job seekers. Nevertheless, in more basic terms, job seekers in remote rural areas largely continued to take the view that new technology could do little to address the more fundamental problems of limited job opportunities within the local economy.

Telephone-based services and job seeking

Most focus group participants in West Lothian were, perhaps understandably, unfamiliar with the Jobcentre Plus agency's 'Jobseeker Direct' telephone helpline. Once again, the proximity of on the ground Jobcentre services appeared to negate the need for ICT-based support systems. None of the seventeen job seekers attending the West Lothian focus groups for young people had used Jobseeker Direct, and only a few were aware of the existence of the service. Levels of awareness were higher amongst '25+' long-term unemployed people, but again only a small minority (two out of a total of fourteen participants across two focus groups) had used the service. This pattern was replicated in other meetings, with one participant each in our focus groups for 'over 50s' and women returners having used Jobseeker Direct.

The small number of people who had used the service cited cost and convenience as their main reasons – although Jobseeker Direct offered no more information than was available through Jobcentre staff, it could allow job seekers to save on time and transport costs by looking for work from home. Those who had experience of Jobseeker Direct generally described the helpline as being user-friendly and helpful, and most users could recall identifying appropriate opportunities through the service. Nevertheless, the overall impression was again one of ICT services operating at the margins. For those residing within travelling distance of on the ground services, the face-to-face contact and routine of attending the Jobcentre in person appears to be preferable to using telephone-based services from home.

Awareness of the Jobseeker Direct service was much higher amongst participants in our Wick focus groups. Almost all of the participants across all three focus groups were aware of Jobseeker Direct, and around half had used the service at some time. Jobseeker Direct was again described as user-friendly, with job seekers commending the courteous and helpful staff manning the service. However, familiar doubts were raised about the ability of the service to assist job seekers into work, given that the helpline operators had access only to the same severely limited pool of local job vacancies that was available to Jobcentre staff. A commonly expressed view was that, much like jobpoints and Internet services, Jobseeker Direct might offer a useful alternative for those wishing to leave the area to find work, but could do little for local job seekers.

The people on the telephone line – they're only giving me information that I can get from the local Jobcentre anyway, or from the papers. There's no additional information. I thought that this was some alternative, but it's not.
(David, 51, unemployed one year, Wick)

If you're willing to move – to move out of your area – then possibly it's of some benefit, otherwise it's not. But given my circumstances, I don't want to move to the central belt [of Scotland]. *Doubtless, if my circumstances had been different, they might have been able to help me.*
(Iain, 63, unemployed two years, Wick)

Sutherland focus group members were in a different position. Residing outwith a realistic travelling distance to their nearest Jobcentre at Wick, job seekers in Sutherland's villages are required to 'phone in' to confirm their availability for work and receive job search advice and information. These regular telephone contacts with Jobcentre staff at Wick, combined with the Jobseeker Direct national telephone helpline and the agency's website, are the main services offered by Jobcentre Plus for unemployed people in Sutherland's remote communities. The telephone is therefore the most important means of delivering services for job seekers in these rural areas.

Many Sutherland job seekers commended the work of Jobcentre Plus staff, whom they saw as making a genuine effort to help, while struggling against the absence of any strong demand for labour in these remote communities. However, a matter of considerable concern for participants in all our Sutherland-based focus groups was the *apparent* progressive withdrawal of 'local' telephone services (provided by staff at the Jobcentre in Wick) and an increasing reliance on the Jobseeker Direct national helpline. Whereas job seekers were previously able to call Jobcentre staff, who would then spend time providing job search services, the impression was that their inquiries were now almost always forwarded to the national helpline. Jobseeker Direct was far less popular with focus group participants, owing to the lack of local knowledge amongst its operators – a crucial failing given the unique problems of distance and remoteness faced by many Sutherland job seekers.

> *A while ago, you used to phone up the Jobcentre at Wick to do a job search and they would do it there. Now they put you through to Jobseeker Direct, and they have no idea about where you live. I told the operator that I was 60 miles from my nearest Jobcentre and she didn't believe me. They were offering me jobs in Fort William* [a journey of over 200 km by road]. *It's the same every week, they just don't know where you are.*
> (Eric, 26, unemployed five months, Brora, Sutherland)

> *They haven't got a clue really where you are. You seem to just get the nearest available line, which could be anywhere. They offer you vacancies anywhere from the Western Isles to Aberdeen. They just don't have a clue – it's a complete waste of time speaking to them to be honest.*
> (Tom, 55, unemployed two years, Bonar Bridge, Sutherland)

> *It happens a lot now when you phone Wick, which is meant to be the local Jobcentre, and you're transferred through to Jobseeker Direct. The last person I was transferred to was in Dundee, and they really don't know about the situation up here.*
> (Alex, 45, unemployed five years, Helmsdale, Sutherland)

Many of these job seekers were sceptical about the benefits of a locally focused job search service, given the more basic problem of a lack of opportunities in Sutherland, but others remained convinced that contact with local Jobcentre professionals was of considerable value. It would appear that these job seekers felt that it was inherently more worthwhile to discuss their employment prospects with advisers who were aware of the local labour market context and knowledgeable about the area's geography. On a practical level, there was also the impression that informal discussions with local Jobcentre staff could flag up opportunities that might not ordinarily be considered by either service provider or client. An exchange between two job seekers participating in the Sutherland conference call focus group illustrates this point.

> *When it comes down to it, it doesn't really matter who tells me there's nothing available. It doesn't really matter if it's a nice lady who I know by name from Wick or an anonymous person somewhere else.*
> (George, 54, unemployed two years, Lochinver, Sutherland)

> *But the difference is, if you speak to someone from Wick and they know about the local area, you can have a chat and they can keep you right, whereas if you speak to someone down South, it gets to you if they haven't got a clue where you are and offer you jobs miles away. It's a complete waste of time, whereas I've never really felt that it's a waste of time phoning Wick.*
> (Alex, 45, unemployed five years, Helmsdale, Sutherland)

> *Yes, I suppose that's a point. The other thing is that they seem to have codes for the jobs you are looking for* [SOC codes used by Jobcentre staff to target clients' job search activities]. *Wick use the same codes for their job searches as the people at Jobseeker Direct. But at Wick they'll check those codes, but they also might also know of other opportunities that have cropped up in the local area that I wouldn't normally be notified of, because it's not included in this code list they have for me. They're more likely to suggest other things that Jobseeker Direct wouldn't.*
> (George, 54, unemployed two years, Lochinver, Sutherland)

In summary, the above findings again demonstrate that whereas ICT-based services for job seekers appear to have had a fairly limited impact in West Lothian, a centrally located, peri-urban labour market with strong formal job search facilities, awareness and use of these services (in this case in the form of telephone helplines) were much more prevalent in remote rural areas. This was particularly the case in Sutherland's more remote communities, where job seekers relied on telephone-based services as their main (and in some cases only) means of contact with the public employment service. However, the experiences of job seekers in Sutherland illustrate how an over-reliance on ICT-based services has the potential to lead to the gradual erosion of direct contact between key public agencies and their clients, adding to the sense of isolation amongst vulnerable groups in remote areas. Many focus group participants had valued the opportunity to speak to advisers who, although not 'local', were based in the northern Highlands and were aware of the problems of distance and geography faced by rural job seekers. The increasing reliance on the Jobseeker Direct national helpline to deliver services to these job seekers raises the danger of severing the link between unemployed people and public employment service professionals whose local knowledge can be valuable, or at the very least reassuring.

There is no doubt that the Jobseeker Direct helpline can efficiently link job seekers who have specific targets and a degree of mobility to a broader range of opportunities. During 2001–02 the service received 4.5 million calls, resulting in almost 4.4 million referrals and 115,000 job entries (DWP, 2002). However, there is evidence that the introduction of the service has had little impact on the regularity with which most unemployed people use Jobcentres, and that the vast majority of users live within 30 minutes travelling distance to their local Jobcentre office (GHK, 2002b). For these people, the Jobseeker Direct service would appear to offer a useful addition to – but not a replacement for – local services. For the minority of job seekers *without* direct access to Jobcentre facilities, the national helpline increasingly represents their main point of contact with the Jobcentre Plus agency, provided *instead of* local services. Yet, as we have seen above, for many unemployed people in rural Sutherland, the 'Direct' approach appears to have marked the transition to an apparently more functional but ultimately less satisfactory job search service.

These findings highlight a fundamental dilemma concerning the increased use of ICT-based services at the national level. ICT has the potential to reduce administrative and other costs, expand personal choice in accessing information (e.g. in terms of time, privacy and location), and provide information that is both broader in scope and more targeted in addressing the needs of specific client groups. However, the drive towards ICT-based services may ignore both the subtleties of information that can be adapted or passed on by staff with local knowledge (especially important in rural areas) and the psychological support or encouragement sometimes required by job seekers who may lack ICT or even simple job search skills, and who may benefit from advice and counselling provided informally by local service providers.

Job search methods used by focus group participants

The potential benefits and limitations of ICT-based job seeking

In rural Sutherland, where telephone helplines form a necessary element in basic public employment services, ICT has an established role in the routine of job seeking for unemployed people. In the same study area, the Internet would appear to act as a convenient job search tool for *some* job seekers. However, in Sutherland and our other study areas, the impact of this form of ICT appears to have been limited in terms of delivering added value for job seekers. In many cases, a lack of appropriate skills and access problems may go some way to explaining job seekers' reluctance to embrace ICT and particularly the Internet as a job search tool (although it should be noted that in all study areas there was reasonably high awareness of the availability of on-line PCs at public facilities such as libraries and community centres). An equally important explanation, especially in Wick and West Lothian, would appear to lie in the availability of local Jobcentre facilities, and the perception that ICT-based services offered few *additional* benefits for job seekers.

Given the continued importance of ICT within the government's policy agenda, particularly in the rural context, we were interested in discussing measures that might help expand the use of new technologies amongst the unemployed, along with any external factors that might continue to limit the take-up of ICT-based services. A small number of job seekers across all the study areas suggested that a more interactive, and proactive, approach to the use of new technologies was required. Focus group participants in Wick and West Lothian noted that the highly detailed information gathered by Jobcentre Plus could be put to good use matching job seekers to vacancies as they arose. Although the Jobcentre Plus agency promotes this form of job matching as a key service for its clients, none of our focus group participants had been contacted by advisers seeking to match them to job opportunities. It was suggested that increased efforts on the part of the agency to make good on its claim that it provides a full job matching service would be useful. Clearly, there is a potential role for ICT in facilitating job matching services and issuing vacancy alerts to clients.

As noted above, focus group participants in Wick and Sutherland also stressed the need for changes to the software that facilitates both the jobpoint and web-based facilities provided by Jobcentre Plus. In small communities where relatively few vacancies arise on a weekly basis, job seekers would clearly find a simple list of jobs-by-area preferable to the searchable, but highly detailed database currently available. (It should be acknowledged, and was by rural focus group participants, that the design of the jobpoint/website software undoubtedly offers benefits for job seekers in busy, urban labour markets seeking to search through large numbers of vacancies.) The idea of a local website, providing less formal 'notice board' type facilities, was welcomed by job seekers in Wick, and particularly Sutherland. Similarly, as noted above, Sutherland-based focus group participants were keen to see the restoration of an easily accessible, *Highlands-based* telephone advice service.

Nevertheless, for many focus group participants the form and content of ICT-based services, and indeed any formal services, remained a marginal issue. Particularly for those in remote rural areas, problems relating to transport, geography and crucially, the lack of local demand for labour, were far more important. Furthermore, within all client groups and areas, there was awareness that informal methods of recruitment and job seeking and particularly social networking can be critical in determining job search success. Again, these issues appeared to be particularly relevant in remote rural communities. It is to these issues that we now turn.

Social networking and job seeking

Focus group participants in all the study areas acknowledged the potential importance of social networks in job seeking, but there was a clear divergence of view between the majority of West Lothian job seekers and those from both the Wick and Sutherland areas (see also Tables 3 and 4 for related results in the first phase research). For those from West Lothian, informal networking was viewed as one potential job search method, but was often not vital to job seekers' efforts to obtain work. Participants in our West Lothian focus groups for young people were particularly unlikely to view informal methods as an efficient way of looking for work. Most young people in our West Lothian groups reported that the majority of their friends and family were in work, but they did not wish to use these connections. In many cases, young job seekers had no desire to follow friends into low quality factory or service jobs. Indeed, there was some evidence of social networks acting as a means of discouraging job seekers from pursuing certain job vacancies, as friends and family warned of low pay and poor conditions.

> *Most of my friends are in work. But what's the point of working in a factory or a warehouse all your life? No danger. It's boring and you'll get no qualifications out of that. There's no way I'm going for that – no chance.*
> (Barry, 19, unemployed six months, West Lothian)

Many young people also expressed concerns that 'using' friends to look for work might damage relationships that were essentially social in nature. Having only recently left school, few of these job seekers had relationships with former colleagues.

Participants in focus groups for women returners and 'adult' long-term unemployed job seekers were more conscious of the potential value of social networks. Yet there remained a reluctance to exploit fully these personal contacts. As was the case with young people, social networks more often operated as a mechanism for warning job seekers to avoid low quality occupations in which friends and former colleagues now found themselves, and again the clash between 'using' contacts to look for work and the values of personal friendship was an issue for some focus group participants.

> *I agree that personal approaches and using people you know is often the best way. But for me it somehow doesn't feel right to use friends or people you used to work with just to look for work.*
> (Mary, 48, unemployed one year, West Lothian)

Long-term unemployed people also tended to view the operation of social networks as a factor contributing to their continued unemployment, rather than as a means of finding their way back into work. There was a general consensus that informal networks were more difficult to maintain as unemployment duration lengthened, and job seekers lost touch with former colleagues and struggled to finance social activities. This view was shared by long-term unemployed people attending focus groups in Wick and Sutherland. However, in these areas the importance of informal recruitment and job search methods was continually stressed by job seekers who saw the operation of social networks in isolated rural labour markets as fundamentally challenging the effectiveness of any formal services for job seekers, including those delivered via ICT.

Despite the presence of job search services on the ground in Wick, focus group participants agreed that informal networking was clearly the single most important method of recruitment and job seeking in that area. A number of focus group participants stressed the importance of personal reputation – 'being known' – and suggested that the long-term unemployed, young people and 'incomers' faced particular problems in (re-)establishing themselves within the local labour market as a result. Job seekers attending focus groups in Sutherland were even more convinced that informal social networks, rather than interventions by public agencies, governed the allocation of jobs in their local communities.

> *It's about getting yourself established and getting to know people, to know where the jobs are. There are jobs, but word of mouth goes a long way. If you know people, you can get a job. It's not what you know, it's who you know. It's as simple as that.*
> (Andrew, 63, unemployed seven months, Lairg, Sutherland)

It was suggested that as a result of the strength of informal social network relations in these communities and the tradition of recruitment by word of mouth, many job vacancies were not communicated to the Jobcentre or advertised by any other formal means. Yet although many long-term unemployed people who participated in focus groups acknowledged that they faced particular problems in accessing informal networks, there was a general acceptance that these traditions were part of rural life, and could be effectively exploited, given a combination of good luck and sound judgement.

> *In smaller communities, if there's anything going people know about them. Some jobs are just sort of arranged beforehand – the person who is going to get the job has already been decided before the vacancy even occurs. These things don't get advertised.*
> (George, 54, unemployed two years, Lochinver, Sutherland)

> *It's always been like that here. You'll not get away from word of mouth, because everybody knows everybody.*
> (Tom, 55, unemployed two years, Bonar Bridge, Sutherland)

> *Yes, some jobs never make it to the Jobcentre – it's all word of mouth. But if you get in there early and speak to someone you can have a good chance.*
> (Alex, 45, unemployed five years, Helmsdale, Sutherland)

Indeed, for some Sutherland job seekers, there was clear value in the operation of informal networks of job seeking and recruitment, even if they, as individuals, had not benefited recently. Social networks were seen as a way of gathering more anecdotal, broad-ranging information about the local labour market, information which could nonetheless be vital in identifying job opportunities. Discussions with friends, neighbours and former colleagues would often touch on current job opportunities, but also more general changes in the local labour market, companies and families moving in and out of the community and potential future vacancies.

> *Everybody knows everyone else and if any vacancies crop up word gets around. If there's something you've missed then somebody will mention about it. There's a sort of an informal job seekers' network. When you talk to people, it's not just a case of finding out what jobs are available. You can find out if someone's leaving their job because they're pregnant or relocating, you can get advance information on companies that are expanding – it's handy to know in advance sometimes.*
> (George, 54, unemployed two years, Lochinver, Sutherland)

An obvious problem associated with the important role played by informal social networking in rural job seeking relates to the marginalisation of formal services for the unemployed, delivered through the public employment service. Participants in our Sutherland focus groups often saw their use of the telephone and Internet-based services provided by Jobcentre Plus as 'going through the motions' or at best as a potentially useful supplementary activity (particularly for those able to travel substantial distances or considering leaving the area). The general view was, however, that the majority of job opportunities were not advertised through the Jobcentre network. It was also suggested by a number of job seekers that those opportunities that were advertised via the Jobcentre still tended to be allocated through personal contacts, with the notification of the vacancy to Jobcentre staff reflecting some larger employers' grudging acknowledgement of equal opportunities legislation, rather than a genuine attempt to open up the recruitment process.

> *If a local job comes up you're not going to see it on a website, you're not even going to see it in a Jobcentre. If somebody knows the right person, then they'll get the job.*
> (Rod, 36, unemployed six months, Lairg, Sutherland)

In summary, job seekers across all the study areas acknowledged, to a greater or lesser extent, the potential importance of informal networking to job search success. However, whereas young people, and even some more experienced job seekers, in West Lothian were reluctant to follow their friends into low quality work, and sometimes balked at 'using' personal relationships to find work, informal networking once again emerged as a crucial element in job seeking in the rural town of Wick and, particularly, Sutherland's remote communities. The vast majority of job seekers in remote rural areas accepted the informality of local job allocation processes as 'the way it has always been', a long-standing practice from which one might benefit or lose, but it was also acknowledged that 'outsiders' – such as young people and the long-term unemployed – tended to struggle more than most to establish or re-establish themselves within these informal networks. Those excluded from informal, social networks may have to rely on formal services provided by Jobcentre Plus as the main element in their job search activities. Given the apparently dominant role of informal networks in job seeking and recruitment in remote communities, the absence of on the ground services for the unemployed and the problems noted by focus group participants regarding the use of ICT-based provision, these disadvantaged job seekers may face considerable additional barriers in identifying appropriate opportunities and so making the transition to work.

Local labour demand and services for the unemployed

An even more profound problem reported by rural job seekers related to the basic lack of employment opportunities within local labour markets. For many focus group participants in Wick and Sutherland, the lack of locally available, appropriate job opportunities could not be separated from the debate regarding the future of services for job seekers in these areas. A minority argued strongly in favour of the expansion of local provision for job seekers, suggesting that the absence of formal Jobcentre and other services led to a depersonalised and ineffective relationship with public employment service professionals.

> *I think it's important.* [At the Jobcentre] *at least you've got a face to face contact. You can talk about other things and that'll give them an idea of what you need, what sort of person you are, what sort of job you might be good at. At the moment it's very impersonal.*
> (Helen, 55, unemployed four weeks, Brora, Sutherland)

As noted above, the majority of focus group participants in both Wick and Sutherland also suggested that they would welcome Internet and telephone-based services that reflected local labour market conditions and provided a 'local focus'. However, many job seekers noted that the local economy was unstable and provided relatively few long-term job opportunities. For these focus group participants, improvements to job search services within local communities or delivered through ICT could not address the more basic problem of a lack of jobs. Indeed, job seekers in Wick and Sutherland often expressed sympathy with Jobcentre staff, whom they perceived as 'doing their best' in extremely difficult circumstances.

> *It must be soul-destroying for those girls at Wick* [Jobcentre staff]. *They know there's no jobs, but they feel they have to go through all these rules about looking for work They say 'Sorry, but I have to tell you about this job' which can be 200 miles away. I take the view that they don't do it because they don't care – they do care. But there's no jobs, but they feel they've got to offer you something. Everybody goes through the motions, but if there ain't any jobs, there ain't any jobs.*
> (Robbie, 45, unemployed two years, Lairg, Sutherland)

The majority of all focus group participants in Wick and Sutherland considered the lack of available job opportunities to be the single most important barrier to work that they faced.[7] Many Sutherland job seekers took the view that the development of locally-based job search services (for instance through an extension of Jobcentre Plus facilities) could offer marginal benefits in terms of convenience, but was unlikely to result in an improvement in their own circumstances.

> *I don't see the point of them coming out here to tell us what we already know – that there are no jobs.*
> (Bill, 48, unemployed six years, Lairg, Sutherland)

> *It would be like rearranging the deckchairs on the Titanic.*
> (Robbie, 45, unemployed two years, Lairg, Sutherland)

> *That's right – the only thing it would do would be to give people somewhere to go to moan about the fact that there is no work.*
> (Rod, 36, unemployed six months, Lairg, Sutherland)

The same problem – the lack of local job opportunities – combined with difficulties in accessing public and private transport was also cited by both Wick and Sutherland job seekers as a crucial factor limiting the impact of any ICT-based services, whatever their content and design features.

> *It sounds great, but number one we need jobs, number two we need transport, forget the Internet.*
> (Robbie, 45, unemployed two years, Lairg, Sutherland)

> *All the technology in the world will not help if the jobs aren't there. It doesn't matter. We could all have PCs at home, be continually on-line looking for jobs, but if there are no jobs in the area, high-technology does nothing at all for you.*
> (Iain, 63, unemployed two years, Wick)

Focus group participants in West Lothian also raised concerns regarding local labour market opportunities, but here job seekers were more often disappointed by the quality of the jobs available. The factory and call centre jobs that, for many job seekers, seemed to dominate vacancies in West Lothian were often viewed as low-paid and a 'dead-end'. However, focus group participants in the West Lothian area were generally less cynical about their long-term employment potential, with those attending our meetings for women returners and young people particularly likely to express a generally 'up-beat' view of their future prospects. The views of focus group participants on the potential for improved job seeking support to deliver access to employment would seem to have broadly reflected the conditions within their local labour markets. For those in remote rural areas such as Wick and Sutherland, areas located at the economic periphery and suffering from the continued decline in primary sector employment, there was an understandable pessimism regarding the extent to which any reform of job search services would improve their long-term job prospects.

Overall, it would appear that, if ICT is to play an important role in delivering services for job seekers in rural areas, the design and content of Internet provision must be such that the new technology can be used to foster social networking as well as merely providing formal vacancy information. Informal networks are crucial to job seeking in rural labour markets – so much so that formal job search services, whether delivered through ICT or in person by staff from key public agencies, are often seen as rather marginal in comparison. The development of web-based services that provide official job search facilities *and* opportunities for informal interaction may be one way of using ICT to bridge the gap between formal services and social networking in rural areas. Job seekers' frustration at the basic lack of opportunities in their local communities will be a more difficult issue to address. The above discussion merely reiterates the need for supply-side policies designed to promote more efficient job seeking, to be combined with innovative demand-side strategies for economic development in rural labour markets.

Lessons from the focus group research: job seekers' attitudes towards ICT

The focus group phase of the research provided a number of insights into the current and potential impact of ICT-based services for job seekers. A range of specific issues arose from the research, relating to: the adaptability of job seekers to the introduction of new technologies; strengths and weaknesses in the design of Jobcentre Plus agency's on-line services; the still relatively marginal role played by all forms of ICT-based provision for job seekers; skills, access and awareness issues that may have affected individuals' ability to engage in Internet-based job seeking; and the manner in which the introduction of ICT-based services can affect the 'personal' aspects of the relationship between agencies such as Jobcentre Plus and their clients.

The introduction of jobpoints in Jobcentres has shown that many unemployed people can adapt to the use of new technology if provided with appropriate support and advice. Indeed, focus group participants' evaluation of the impact of jobpoints tended to be measured and well-balanced. Concerns were raised about the limitations of the software, which rarely allows job seekers to pursue opportunities independently of Jobcentre staff. For those in rural areas characterised by small pools of job opportunities, and those looking for general, unskilled work, there was a feeling that the new technology could over-complicate the job search process, preventing job seekers from searching quickly across a range of different local vacancies (one of the few benefits of the preceding cards and boards system). Yet for many job seekers, the privacy and autonomy afforded by the jobpoint terminals marked a step forward from the traditional cards and boards approach.

The same concerns raised by some job seekers regarding the introduction of jobpoints were also relevant to Internet-based services. While those residing in remote rural areas not served by Jobcentre facilities were much more likely to use the Internet to look for work, it emerged that the design of Jobcentre Plus agency's on-line job search site was better suited to the needs of those trying to navigate large urban labour markets. Rural job seekers again complained that the complex, searchable database provided by the Jobcentre Plus (designed to enable clients to target opportunities by area, sector and occupation) tended to over-complicate the search process in remote communities where a simple list of all local job opportunities may have been more helpful. However, it should be noted that these criticisms were balanced by a generally favourable response to the Jobcentre Plus website in terms of its clarity and usability. Job seekers offered constructive suggestions for the improvement of Internet-based services:

- websites should have a local, as well as national, focus
- more detailed information on pay, working hours and conditions should be provided, and
- the facilities available through some private sector employment agency sites should be extended to the services provided by public agencies such as Jobcentre Plus (e.g. job seekers should be able to save personal profiles, receive vacancy bulletins and submit CVs to be perused by prospective recruiters).

Nevertheless, an important finding also relates to the still relatively marginal role played by all forms of ICT-based provision for job seekers. The majority of focus group participants in all areas and particularly those in West Lothian, which is well served by Jobcentre facilities, rarely or never used ICT as a job search tool. In the remote rural town of Wick, none of our focus group participants used the Internet regularly (i.e. weekly) to look for work, and only a small minority used it on a more infrequent basis. Although those in the even more remote Sutherland labour market, which has no Jobcentre facilities, were more likely to use the Internet, those involved in regular web-based job seeking did not even form a majority amongst those who had home access to the Internet.

For some of these job seekers, there were skills, access and awareness issues that may have affected their ability to engage in Internet-based job seeking. But it was also clear that many focus group participants believed that there was little need to add Internet job seeking to their current activities. In the peri-urban West Lothian labour market, most focus group participants saw Internet-based job seeking as offering few benefits in addition to attending local Jobcentre facilities, a view that was shared by many of those in Wick. In Sutherland, despite the absence of formal Jobcentre facilities, there was scepticism as to the added value offered by the Internet as a job search tool. The Jobcentre Plus website was viewed as offering access to the same severely limited pool of local job opportunities as the Jobseeker Direct telephone helpline. In both cases, job seekers in remote rural areas took the view that the introduction of these ICT-based services had had a very limited impact owing to the basic lack of opportunities in local labour markets and the important role of informal networks, which meant that most job vacancies were not subject to any form of formal advertising. The role of informal social networks, and their potential in limiting the value of any new services for job seekers, was an important theme to emerge from both the Wick and Sutherland focus groups (in contrast to the West Lothian focus groups, where the issue was acknowledged, but not considered crucial).

Locally-focused, web-based facilities may be one way of encouraging the development of more open methods of job seeking and recruitment in rural labour markets. An opening out of these processes, long dominated by word of mouth and informal networking, is important for two reasons. First, vulnerable groups, such as those without strong work records (e.g. the long-term unemployed and young people) are routinely disadvantaged by the operation of networks, which allocate jobs on the principle of 'knowing the right people'. Second, interventions by key public agencies seeking to assist job seekers into work would appear to be consistently undermined by the manner in which many vacancies are not formally advertised. There may therefore be a role for local websites which provide opportunities for community networking and discussion, and a virtual space where job seekers and recruiters can share information. Such community-focused, web-based services may also be useful in providing the general, 'local jobs lists' requested by rural job seekers.

Finally, the focus group research raised questions about the manner in which the introduction of ICT-based services can affect the 'personal' aspects of the link between agencies such as Jobcentre Plus and their clients. The apparent increasing dependence of Jobcentre Plus on its national Jobseeker Direct helpline to provide information services in Sutherland appeared to have undermined the relationship between the agency and many of its clients who attended our focus groups. Although sceptical about the ability of formal service providers to provide access to work (owing to the external factors noted above) many Sutherland job seekers had valued the opportunity to discuss their situation with service professionals based in the northern Highlands, who had 'local knowledge' of the problems faced by unemployed people in remote rural communities. The experience of these job seekers highlights the manner in which ICT has the capacity both to improve the basic accessibility of services at the local level (by providing a telephone helpline in communities not served by facilities on the ground), and to act as a centralising force, enabling policy makers to retain established service centres and deliver services for isolated communities 'remotely'.

The transition to a national helpline dealing with job search inquiries from these areas has left many already disadvantaged job seekers feeling increasingly isolated. In recent years, the telephone helpline operated from Wick Jobcentre, manned by well-informed local staff, has provided the main (and in some cases only) regular direct contact between Jobcentre Plus and its clients in remote areas of Sutherland. It will be a matter of concern if this service is to be progressively withdrawn. In more general terms, there may be an important role for telephone helplines in delivering information services for job seekers in remote rural labour markets, but the lessons of our focus groups would appear to be that such services are most effective if they combine access to regional and national datasources with opportunities for job seekers to interact with local service providers.

4 Conclusions and implications for research and policy

This final chapter brings together the conclusions of the study and sets out implications for policy. First, it compares the differing attitudes and experiences of job seekers between client groups and across remote rural and peri-urban areas. Next it considers both barriers and benefits associated with ICT-based services for job seekers. Finally, we discuss implications for future policy and research, in terms of developing services for job seekers and bridging the 'digital divide'.

Summary of findings

This project combined a comparative, quantitative analysis of datasets developed from two individual surveys of job seekers with in-depth, qualitative focus group research. This mixed methodology has proved highly effective in identifying and comparing ICT access and use amongst the unemployed in the study areas, and then following up in detail some specific issues concerning job seekers' attitudes and experiences of new technologies. A caveat should be acknowledged: all the respondents participating in the job seeker surveys and focus groups had thus far been *unsuccessful* in finding work. There is a clear need for more detailed research on the relationship between ICT access and skills and job search success. Nevertheless, the views and experiences of currently unemployed job seekers – the client group targeted by government labour market inclusion strategies that increasingly promote the role of ICT – remain of considerable interest in evaluating this approach to policy.

Our research sought to address two key questions facing policy makers and service providers tackling labour market disadvantage in both rural and urban areas:

- What are the potential benefits and barriers associated with the delivery of services for job seekers through the use of ICT-based systems, and particularly the Internet, in rural and other labour markets?
- What is the nature and extent of the 'digital divide' affecting unemployed job seekers and what policies are required to address this problem?

ICT and job seeking: comparing study areas and client groups

The findings of this study highlight the importance of labour market geography in providing the context for the job seeking activities of unemployed people. The study compared the attitudes and experiences of those looking for work in West Lothian, a centrally located, well-connected, peri-urban area, with others in Wick, a small, remote rural town, and Sutherland, with its very remote communities scattered across a large rural area. Our survey research illustrated that, in the peri-urban West Lothian area, job seekers tended to be highly dependent on formal services 'on the ground', provided by the public employment service, Jobcentre Plus. This was less the case in the remote town of Wick. Job seekers in Sutherland, where no formal services are available on the ground, rarely travelled to visit their nearest Jobcentre (in Wick).

However, in Sutherland and Wick, informal, social networking emerged as a crucial element in job seeking. Job seekers took the view that informal methods of recruiting and job seeking were an accepted part of rural life, but it was also acknowledged that the informality of these processes, and the way that both employers and job seekers often by-passed formal service providers such as Jobcentre Plus, could add to the disadvantage experienced by those without a strong foothold in the labour market (such as young people, women returners and the long-term unemployed).

It is clear that the Internet remains marginal to the job search activities of the majority of unemployed people. The use of the Internet as a job search tool was much more prevalent in the remote rural Sutherland TTWA than in either Wick or West Lothian (both areas served by Jobcentre facilities). Yet even in Sutherland's more remote areas, the Internet was of relatively marginal importance to job seekers (although telephone helplines were used much more extensively here than in the other study areas). For those residing near to Jobcentre facilities, web-based job seeking and telephone helplines were viewed as being likely to add little of value to the existing services offered by Jobcentre Plus. For those in more remote areas, the perceived lack of local job opportunities, the importance of informal networks and the absence of locally focused, web-based resources discouraged the use of the Internet to look for work.

However, any discussion of the potential role of ICT in delivering services for job seekers must acknowledge the extent of the digital divide that continues to affect many unemployed people, and especially disadvantaged groups. The majority of job seekers surveyed in all study areas did not have access to the Internet, and many reported low levels of ICT skills. Our survey research illustrated that, within the general unemployed population, Internet access and use was largely the preserve of the higher skilled and those in higher household-income bands. Meanwhile, on the other side of the digital divide that separates job seekers, the unskilled, the unqualified and those with low household incomes were much less likely to use the Internet or have the levels of access, skills or awareness required to exploit the opportunities associated with web-based services. The reality is that the ability of unemployed job seekers to gain access to and use ICT and the Internet reflects the degree of disadvantage already experienced by individuals and groups. It is therefore essential that policies to promote ICT use are developed alongside strategies to address this digital divide, so guarding against the danger that the most disadvantaged may be left behind by the drive towards ICT-based services.

ICT-based job seeking: barriers and benefits

In all areas, a lack of access to ICT, and specifically the Internet (especially at home), along with limited ICT skills were important factors explaining the reluctance of many unemployed people to use the Internet to facilitate job seeking. However, there was evidence that skill barriers could be overcome in many cases – job seekers were generally aware of the increasing importance of ICT skills, and were willing to consider training in this area.

Job seekers also demonstrated their adaptability when faced with the introduction of new technologies. The recent introduction of jobpoints (which use web-based technology to link Jobcentre clients with a national jobs database) met with a mostly positive response, with many Jobcentre users welcoming the enhanced sense of privacy and autonomy provided by the terminals. Where there was criticism, it tended to be constructive, with some job seekers arguing for changes to the software design to enable easier browsing across occupations and local areas – a reform that would be particularly helpful for unskilled workers and those living in rural areas with small pools of local job opportunities. Similar concerns were raised about the Jobcentre Plus website, which shares its software design with jobpoints. Although the site itself was viewed as user-friendly, rural job seekers again argued for the introduction of an accessible 'local list' of *all* available vacancies, to operate alongside the service's more sophisticated national database system.

One way in which ICT already plays an important role in the delivery of job search services involves the local and national telephone helplines that link job seekers in remote rural areas (such as Sutherland's more isolated communities) with Jobcentre Plus advisers. Telephone helpline services clearly have the potential to deliver easily accessible information and advice to unemployed people in communities where the establishment of Jobcentre facilities may not be feasible. However, evidence from our Sutherland focus groups suggested that an over-reliance on standardised forms of new technology, such as centralised *national* telephone helplines, may add to the sense of isolation experienced by job seekers in remote rural areas. (Many Sutherland job seekers contrasted the 'one size fits all' approach of the national Jobseeker Direct helpline with the local knowledge, in terms of labour market geography and range of vacancies, offered by telephone advisers based at their nearest Jobcentre at Wick.)

Our focus groups in rural Wick and Sutherland also highlighted the more fundamental limitations of the new technology. The lack of job opportunities in relatively depressed, remote rural labour markets seems to have produced a degree of cynicism amongst job seekers, and particularly the long-term unemployed, who often view their interactions with service providers, whatever the means of service delivery, as 'going through the motions'. Furthermore, as noted above, for many job seekers in these areas, informal networks were considered a more useful source of vacancy information than any form of formal services (delivered through ICT or in person). The importance of informal methods of job seeking and recruitment in remote rural labour markets reflects the traditions and practicalities of economic relations in small communities, and these practices have been reinforced by the absence of formal services on the ground. If ICT is to have a greater impact in these areas, it must be delivered through mechanisms and in ways that tap into these established conventions around recruitment and job seeking.

Does ICT and particularly the Internet have a role in delivering services for job seekers in rural and other areas? Owing to convenience or necessity, those in remote rural areas characterised by weak formal service infrastructures were generally more likely to use ICT in various forms. The general acceptance amongst these and other job seekers of the spread of ICT as a means of providing information in Jobcentres and delivering 'remote' services can be built on by public agencies dealing with the unemployed. On the other hand, the research reported here suggests that further measures will be required to support individuals and communities if ICT is to add value to services for job seekers, especially in rural areas. Finally, the more profound problems of labour demand identified by job seekers in depressed rural labour markets will be more difficult to address. These issues are, however, beyond the scope of this report.

Implications for policy

Developing ICT-based services for job seekers
ICT already plays a growing role in the delivery of services for job seekers through the official website operated by Jobcentre Plus, computerised jobpoints in Jobcentres and local and national telephone helplines. There is the potential for ICT-based solutions to play an even greater role in the delivery of job search services, especially in communities with weak formal service infrastructures on the ground. To this end, a number of lessons for future policy can be drawn from the above research.

Website content and design
The manner in which job seekers seem to have adapted to the new jobpoint technology, with strong support from Jobcentre staff, arguably bodes well for the continued development of ICT-based services. Jobcentre Plus may be able to build on the goodwill towards this innovation, and so encourage ICT use in general, by addressing a number of issues. Although the software design for jobpoints is useful for those seeking to target their job search precisely by occupation and area, a more flexible approach would offer benefits for those

residing in rural areas characterised by small job pools (and unskilled workers in all areas). A system that allows general browsing across a broad range of job-types (e.g. all unskilled jobs in a specific geographical area), as well as access to the current highly specified database, would be welcomed by many rural job seekers. These changes are more than a matter of convenience. A more flexible jobpoint system, which also allows users to browse its jobs database in a way that better reflects how they actually look for work, may encourage job seekers to broaden their search strategies to include occupations and sectors that otherwise might not be considered.

Similar changes would also make the Jobcentre Plus website more user-friendly for many. Other moves towards genuinely interactive Internet services may attract even more job seekers. Web-based resources have the capacity to offer a range of service options, from recruitment and job search sites where individuals can save their search profiles and CVs, to on-line application processes, to e-mail vacancy bulletins targeted at specific job seeker newsgroups. Such services, already provided by employment agencies operating in the private sector, may also benefit the unemployed clients of public sector service providers. At the most basic level, there is a need for job search resources that provide sufficiently detailed information on the pay, conditions, working hours and location, so as to allow job seekers to make an informed choice at the outset of the application process.

In all of these areas, there is scope for improvement in the operation of currently available web-based job search services. Future reforms to the design and content of Internet services currently provided by Jobcentre Plus and other public agencies should therefore be informed by a number of defining principles:

- Services should be user-friendly and easily understandable, even for Internet novices.
- Vacancy information should be sufficiently detailed to allow users to make an informed choice as to whether they wish to progress with an application at the outset of the job search process.
- The design of search services should allow for the storing of job seeker profiles, so that users are not required to input the same information repeatedly when carrying out a number of searches.
- Job search services should reflect the needs and common practices of users (for example by enabling job seekers to browse across an extensive range of vacancies and focus their search by area rather than occupation), but continue to enable users to adopt new approaches (for example by providing access to national and international vacancy databases, allowing job seekers to extend their search area).

Locally-focused ICT resources

Another solution may involve the development (possibly by Jobcentre Plus, local authorities and other local agencies) of locally or community-focused web-based resources – a form of provision that may be particularly valuable in rural areas characterised by weak formal service infrastructures. As noted above, in these areas the operation of informal networks can add to the exclusion experienced by some disadvantaged job seeker groups. Locally-focused, web-based resources may have the capacity to provide a 'virtual space' where these and other job seekers can share information, post CVs and job search profiles, connect with recruiting employers, and quickly view a broad range of local vacancies. If effective locally-focused websites can be established, and job seekers and employers are encouraged (and if necessary trained) to use these resources, ICT may have an important role to play in bridging the gap between the informal networking that dominates recruitment and job seeking in rural labour markets and the formal ICT services and resources offered by public agencies like Jobcentre Plus.

Telephone helplines

There is some evidence that 'remote' ICT-based services, which do not respond to local labour market circumstances, have the capacity to further disadvantage job seekers in rural communities. The Jobseeker Direct telephone helpline offers a convenient supplementary service for those who have access to a range of alternative information sources, but for some job seekers in Sutherland's remote rural communities, the extensive use of the national helpline to deliver job search services tended to add to their sense of isolation, and *at times* resulted in unsatisfactory advice. Here, as in other areas, if ICT-based provision is to be effective, it must retain a local dimension, or risk dislocating vulnerable groups and communities from the high quality services that Jobcentre Plus and other public agencies are committed to providing. Where possible, job seekers in areas not serviced by local Jobcentre or other facilities on the ground should therefore have access to telephone and web-based services that, to some extent, retain a 'local' profile, and offer a degree of local knowledge.

Bridging the digital divide

There remain important barriers to the expansion of the role of ICT-based services for job seekers. First, and most obvious, there is a need for further measures to tackle the digital divide experienced by many unemployed job seekers. Unemployed people who are already disadvantaged in terms of skills, educational attainment and income are clearly less likely to have the access and skills required to benefit from using ICT (and particularly the Internet) as a job search tool. The shift towards web-based services risks leaving these individuals behind, unless they are able to receive adequate training and support through accessible local services.

Yet job seekers have shown themselves to be adaptable to the introduction of new technologies, and an expansion of community-based ICT facilities may lead some individuals to broaden their job search via web-based resources provided by Jobcentre Plus and others. An expansion in community ICT facilities need not imply large-scale investment in 'a Jobcentre in every village'. Existing community resources – such as schools, libraries and community centres – have been successfully converted for additional use as ICT centres in many areas. Furthermore, in smaller communities in the Scottish Highlands (including some villages in Caithness and Sutherland) the local authority has recently developed general purpose 'service points', staffed by advisers offering guidance on benefits and local services, which could be adapted to host Internet access areas or remote Jobcentre Plus jobpoint terminals.

There may be benefits in seeking to encourage these trends, especially in rural areas without Jobcentre facilities, by at least partially focusing the work of new community ICT centres on providing access services for the unemployed. The development of work and training-focused ICT centres may be best achieved through the formation of new partnerships involving *all* the relevant local policy actors, such as Jobcentre Plus, local authorities and Local Enterprise Companies. Such partnership-based approaches would add value by enabling the pooling of expertise, information and intelligence, and physical, financial and human resources. Given the increasing acceptance of the importance of accessible services to social inclusion in rural areas, the development of community ICT facilities would appear to 'fit' with the current policy agenda on accessibility and rural development.[8]

Community ICT facilities, offering training and advice provided by professional project staff alongside an emphasis on peer support, may be able to combine the best elements of informal networking (so important in rural labour markets) and formal job search services. Such facilities would be well placed to link with community-focused web-based resources, which (as discussed above) may have the potential to provide added value by offering access to national job search databases, but also local jobs listings and 'virtual spaces' where employers, job seekers and service professionals can share information and interact on a more informal basis. In this way, ICT-based services and community technology facilities may have a future role in 'opening up' the informal networks that can contribute to the exclusion of disadvantaged rural job seekers and undermine the efforts of service providers delivering access to employment policies. However, service providers will need to convince both job seekers and employers of the added value offered by such exercises in 'virtual networking'. Research in Wick and Sutherland has demonstrated that even larger employers can tend to rely on fairly narrow networks of informal contacts when recruiting.[9] Furthermore, there will remain an incentive for some (especially those operating within the informal economy) to retain word of mouth as their primary means of communication about jobs.

Finally, policies to develop new services for job seekers (whether virtual or in 'real life') must connect with the broader agenda for rural economic development. Supply-side policies will only gain credibility amongst job seekers and employers if they are linked to longer-term strategies to encourage exogenous investment and endogenous development. In the more immediate term, there may be considerable benefits in more clearly linking ICT and community-based transport policies. Access to transport and problems of distance continue to represent major barriers to work for many job seekers, and especially those in remote rural areas. Recent attempts to develop demand-responsive transport systems in rural areas (which rely on technology-based solutions to model local transport provision) may be strengthened by links with parallel programmes seeking to deploy ICT to connect job seekers with employers and service providers.[10] Without further support for strategies to stimulate labour demand in rural labour markets, and community-based initiatives to help rural job seekers overcome problems of distance and transport access, service providers will continue to struggle to link their unemployed clients with a pool of local vacancies that is likely to remain severely limited in terms of numbers and range of occupations.

Concluding remarks and areas for further research

Given the currently relatively limited impact of ICT (and particularly the Internet) on job seeking, measures to promote technology-based services may prove to be part of a medium- to long-term policy agenda. Further research is required to establish the link between access and use of new technologies and job search success, and the most effective strategies for implementing ICT-based services in rural and other communities. This may involve further research with both job seekers and employers; the co-operation of the latter group will be essential to any attempt to use ICT to 'open up' informal job search and recruiting networks.

The concerns raised by focus groups regarding the potential for 'remote' ICT-based services to add to the sense of exclusion felt by some vulnerable people in isolated areas also merit further research, so that we can establish how best to balance the expansion of services delivered through ICT and the Internet, with the need for local community facilities to support job seekers in rural areas. At a more fundamental level, a key question for future research relates to how policy makers will strike the balance between designing ICT services to *match* how people actually look for work, and designing ICT services that help people to *change* how they look for work – i.e. should the technology reflect how people currently act, or be used in an attempt to change their behaviour?

There is some evidence that ICT has the potential to play an important role in linking all job seekers (and particularly those in remote rural areas) with more and *more accessible* information. ICT-based services for job seekers may have the capacity to enable recipients to develop new skills, access information on employment and training, extend their social networks and communicate their needs to service providers and policy makers more effectively. The barriers remain significant, but for rural labour markets with weak public service infrastructures and other disadvantaged areas, local, community-focused ICT, both on-line and 'on the ground', may in future offer one way forward in delivering services for unemployed job seekers.

Notes

1 See for example, McQuaid (1997); Chapman *et al.* (1998); Monk *et al.* (1999); Rugg and Jones (1999); US Department of Commerce (1999); Cartmel and Furlong (2000); Pavis *et al.* (2000).

2 Other public Internet job search services include the Careers Scotland and the European Employment Services (EURES) websites, which allow broad searches.

3 The ILO definition of unemployment covers people who are: not in employment, want a job, have actively sought work in the previous four weeks and are available to start work within the next fortnight; or, not in employment and have accepted a job, which they are waiting to start in the next fortnight.

4 During the period when the responses for the first phase research were gathered in Wick and Sutherland (November–December 2000), claimant unemployment was estimated at 7.0 per cent and 10.6 per cent respectively for the two Highland TTWAs, compared with a Scottish national average of 5.0 per cent. In contrast, at the time of the first phase of West Lothian fieldwork (May 2001), local claimant unemployment was estimated at 3.8 per cent, below the then Scottish average of 4.2 per cent. At the outset of the second phase fieldwork (July–November 2002) West Lothian's claimant unemployment stood at 4.2 per cent, compared with 5.2 per cent and 5.8 per cent respectively in the Wick and Sutherland TTWAs, with the Scottish average standing at 4.1 per cent (source: NOMIS at www.nomisweb.co.uk). Note that the unemployment rates given above are based on 'workforce' calculations used at the time, but now discontinued as a measure of local unemployment by the Office for National Statistics. These figures were based on an estimate of the number of local workforce jobs plus the number of non-employed people of working age as a denominator to calculate local unemployment rates. This method (which failed to take into account the impact of commuting) has been replaced by residence-based figures, which use a denominator of all people of working age within the relevant geographical boundary. However, residence-based unemployment statistics for the Wick and Sutherland TTWAs are not currently available through the Office for National Statistics. Accordingly, the statistics provided are the only available *comparative* data relating to unemployment in the study areas during the relevant time periods.

5 The eight-fold geographical classification used by the *Scottish Household Survey* (Scottish Executive, 2001c) is:

- *the four cities* (settlements over 125,000)
- *other urban areas* (settlements 10,000–125,000)
- *accessible small towns* (settlements between 3,000 and 10,000 and within a 30-minute drive from a settlement of 10,000 or more)
- *remote small towns* (settlements sized between 3,000 and 10,000 and between 30 and 60 minutes from a settlement of 10,000 or more)
- *very remote small towns* (settlements sized between 3,000 and 10,000 and over 60 minutes from a settlement of 10,000 or more)
- *accessible rural areas* (settlements of less than 3,000 and within 30 minutes from a settlement of 10,000 or more)
- *remote rural areas* (settlements of less than 3,000 and 30–60 minutes from a settlement of 10,000 or more)
- *very remote rural areas* (settlements of less than 3,000 and over 60 minutes from a settlement of 10,000 or more).

6 See Ashworth and Youngs (2001). See also Speak and Graham (2000) for a discussion of barriers to access to communications technologies in marginalised neighbourhoods.

7 See Lindsay *et al.* (2003) for similar findings concerning the first phase of the research in Wick and Sutherland.

8 See Farrington and Farrington (2002) for a general discussion of the impact of service accessibility on social inclusion. See also Hope *et al.* (2000) for a discussion of services in rural Scotland and Rennie *et al.* (2002) for a discussion of best practice in rural service provision.

9 Lindsay *et al.* (2003) found that both small and large-scale employers in the Wick and Sutherland areas largely depended on informal methods of recruitment. Several employers suggested that in small communities 'word of mouth' was the best means of screening potential employees. Newspaper and Jobcentre notifications were seen as a way of communicating the existence of vacancies, but word of mouth and personal recommendation often still ensured the appointment of what employers considered to be the 'right person'.

10 See Commission for Integrated Transport (2001) for a discussion of the potential benefits of demand-responsive transport in rural areas.

References

Ashworth, K. and Youngs, R. (2001) *Leaving JSA for Part-time Work.* DWP In-house Report 77. London: Department for Work and Pensions

Cartmel, F. and Furlong, A. (2000) *Youth Unemployment in Rural Areas.* York: YPS for the Joseph Rowntree Foundation

Chapman, P., Phimister, E., Shucksmith, M., Upward, R. and Vera-Toscano, E. (1998) *Poverty and Exclusion in Rural Britain: the dynamics of low income and employment.* York: YPS for the Joseph Rowntree Foundation

Coleman, N., Jeeawody, F. and Wapshott, J. (2002) *Electronic Government at the Department for Work and Pensions: attitudes to electronic methods of conducting benefit business.* DWP Research Report 176. London: Department for Work and Pensions

Commission for Integrated Transport (2001) *Study of European Best Practice in the Delivery of Integrated Transport.* Report on stage 3: Transferability, at: www.cfit.gov.uk/research/

DEFRA (Department for Environment, Food and Rural Affairs) (2000) *Our Countryside: the future. A fair deal for rural England.* London: HMSO

DfEE (Department for Education and Employment) (1999) *Improving Adult Literacy and Numeracy – A Fresh Start.* London: DfEE

DTI (Department for Trade and Industry) (2000) *Closing the Digital Divide: information and communication technologies in deprived areas.* London: HMSO

DWP (Department for Work and Pensions) (2002) *The Employment Service Annual Report and Accounts, 2001–02.* London: DWP

Farrington, J. and Farrington, C. (2002) 'Rural accessibility and social inclusion: towards conceptualisation and analysis', paper presented at Conference of Anglo-German Geographers, Thurnau, 5–7 September

GHK (2002a) *Early Views on the Internet Job Bank.* Employment Service Research Report 109. Sheffield: Employment Service

GHK (2002b) *Jobseeker Direct Customer Satisfaction Survey.* Sheffield: Employment Service

Graham, S. (2002) 'Bridging urban digital divides? Urban polarisation and information and communications technologies', *Urban Studies* Vol. 39, No. 1, pp. 33–56

Hope, S., Anderson, S. and Sawyer, B. (2000) *The Quality of Rural Services in Scotland.* Edinburgh: Scottish Executive Central Research Unit

ILO (International Labour Organisation) (2001) *World Employment Report 2001: life at work in the information economy.* Geneva: International Labour Organisation

Lindsay, C., McCracken, M. and McQuaid, R.W. (2003) 'Unemployment duration and employability in remote rural labour markets', *Journal of Rural Studies,* Vol. 19, No. 2, pp. 87–200.

McQuaid, R.W. (1997) 'Local Enterprise Companies and rural development', *Journal of Rural Studies,* Vol. 13, No. 2, pp. 197–212.

Monk, S., Dunn, J., Fitzgerald, M. and Hodge, I. (1999) *Finding Work in Rural Areas: barriers and bridges.* York: YPS for the Joseph Rowntree Foundation

OECD (Organisation for Economic Co-operation and Development) (2000) *Measuring the ICT Sector.* Paris: OECD

Pavis, S., Platt S. and Hubbard, G. (2000) *Young People in Rural Scotland: pathways to social inclusion and exclusion.* York: YPS for the Joseph Rowntree Foundation

Rennie, F., Greller W. and MacKay, M. (2002) *Review of International Best Practice in Service Delivery to Remote and Rural Areas.* Edinburgh: Scottish Executive Central Research Unit

Rugg, J. and Jones, A. (1999) *Getting a Job, Finding a Home: rural youth transitions*. Bristol: The Policy Press for the Joseph Rowntree Foundation

Scottish Executive (2000) *Rural Scotland: a new approach*. Edinburgh: Stationery Office Scotland

Scottish Executive (2001a) *Adult Literacy and Numeracy in Scotland*. Edinburgh: Stationery Office Scotland

Scottish Executive (2001b) *Digital Inclusion: connecting Scotland's people*. Edinburgh: Stationery Office Scotland

Scottish Executive (2001c) *Scotland's People: Results from the 1999/2000 Scottish Household Survey*, Technical Report. Edinburgh: Stationery Office Scotland

Speak, S. and Graham, S. (2000) *Service Not Included: social implications of private sector service restructuring in marginalised neighbourhoods*. Bristol: The Policy Press for the Joseph Rowntree Foundation

United States Department of Commerce (1999) *The Emerging Digital Economy II*, at: http://www.ecommerce.gov/ede/ede2.pdf

Van Winden, W. (2001) 'The end of social exclusion? On information technology policy as a key to social inclusion in large European cities', *Regional Studies*, Vol. 35, No. 9, pp. 861–77